CH00894904

Easy Halogen
Cookbook

Easy Halogen
Cookbook

Quick, simple recipes to help get the most out of your halogen oven

Maryanne Madden

hamlyn

An Hachette UK Company
www.hachette.co.uk

First published in Great Britain in 2011 by
Hamlyn, a division of Octopus Publishing Group Ltd
Endeavour House
189 Shaftesbury Avenue
London
WC2H 8JY
www.octopusbooks.co.uk

Maryanne Madden asserts the moral right to be identified
as the author of this work

ISBN 978-0-600-62234-5

A CIP catalogue record for this book is available from the
British Library

Printed and bound in China

10 9 8 7 6 5 4 3 2 1

NOTES

Read your halogen oven manual before you begin and
preheat the halogen oven if required according to the
manufacturer's instructions. Because halogen ovens vary
slightly from manufacturer to manufacturer, check recipe
timings with the manufacturer's directions for a recipe
using the same ingredients.

Standard level spoon measurements are used in all recipes.
1 tablespoon = one 15 ml spoon
1 teaspoon = one 5 ml spoon

Both imperial and metric measurements have been given
in all recipes. Use one set of measurements only and not
a mixture of both.

Eggs should be medium unless otherwise stated.
The Department of Health advises that eggs should
not be consumed raw. This book contains dishes made
with raw or lightly cooked eggs. It is prudent for more
vulnerable people, such as pregnant and nursing mothers,
invalids, the elderly, babies and young children, to avoid
uncooked or lightly cooked dishes made with eggs. Once
prepared, these dishes should be kept refrigerated and
used promptly.

Milk should be full fat unless otherwise stated.

Contents

Introduction

We're all looking for easy solutions to save time and effort in the kitchen. Halogen ovens are perhaps the most effective way to ensure a stress-free way of cooking and with the right recipes and know-how, even novice cooks will be converted to this super-speedy way of preparing meals.

Halogen ovens cook much more quickly than conventional ovens. You simply place everything in one bowl or use the handy tiered racks to create fantastic meals with the switch of a button. But for many of us a new appliance can be daunting and it takes a while to become familiar with the settings and timings before you can really get the most out of your purchase.

Here's where this simple-to-follow cookbook will come in handy. With 80 easy and delicious recipes, you'll learn the basic techniques that can help you achieve just about any type of meal, including delicious cakes and puddings, succulent roasted joints of meat, home-made chips, crispy baked potatoes, stews, risottos, pasta and pizzas.

Most halogen ovens will come with instructions and a handful of recipes; this book provides a full range of ideas to make halogen cooking a way of life. The recipes are clear and straightforward – helping you to achieve maximum results with minimum effort. So whether you are a first-time cook, a student, trying to balance a busy family schedule, or looking for a convenient way to cook meals for one, this indispensable recipe collection will help you to master the know-how and get cooking today.

Saving on every level

A halogen oven:

- Cuts cooking time by up to 40 per cent.
- Saves energy in two ways: by using lower temperatures to cook and through the reduction of overall cooking time.
- Achieves evenly-cooked food with none of the hot and cold spots you get with microwave cooking.
- Can both seal in juices and keep food moist on the inside, whilst achieving a brown and crisp effect on the outside. It will not make food soggy or dry it out like even the most modern microwave ovens sometimes do.
- Drains away fat from the tiered racks giving you healthier dinners.
- Is portable, compact and suitable for every size of kitchen.
- Means there is no need to defrost. Food can be cooked directly from the freezer. You can clean and season your meat before freezing and then it's ready to go when you need it.
- Has a clear bowl which allows you to monitor the results as you go along and not waste heat and get all hot and bothered from constantly having to open the oven.

- There is also less need to turn the contents when cooking as everything is cooked evenly and thoroughly due it being a fan-assisted oven.
- As if it couldn't get any better, a halogen oven usually has a self-clean function and the glass bowl can be lifted out easily for wiping clean, so there is no need to worry about who will do the washing up afterwards.

All about halogen ovens

A halogen oven uses an innovative combination of powerful halogen lighting and convection. The infrared halogen element found in the oven heats up almost instantly. This reduces the time the oven is on prior to cooking, and due to the unique fan-assisted air circulation, food cooks evenly without the need for turning. Halogen ovens are generally supplied with the following equipment:

- 1 glass bowl
- 1 base stand
- 1 glass lid with halogen element and power cord.
- 2 steel racks
- Steel handles – for safe removal of racks

By using the multiple racks, or simply placing a cooking dish inside, you can cook in much the same way as a conventional oven – but much more effectively. You can cook a whole meal for a family and still have lots of room for vegetables; or it's perfect for smaller meals or those people who are cooking for one, without the need for heating a whole conventional oven.

Getting started

1. Place the glass bowl on the metal base (remembering to do this on a secure kitchen worktop or table).
2. The metal racks then sit one on top of the other, inside the glass bowl.
3. Next, simply place the lid on the glass bowl and push the handle down to lock it.
4. Plug the lead into a nearby socket.
5. Turn the timer clockwise to select the required time. The power light will now be on.
6. Turn the temperature dial clockwise to the required temperature and the light will then come on.
7. When the oven has reached the required temperature the light will turn off.
8. The temperature light will come back on again if the temperature falls, and this will show that the oven is heating up again.
9. When the food is ready (usually indicated by the bell), remove the food from the glass bowl using the steel handles.
10. The lid will now be extremely hot, therefore do not place it directly on your kitchen worktop.

Cleaning a halogen oven

Many halogen ovens have a self-cleaning function which can be used as follows:

1. Fill the glass bowl half full with hot water.
2. Push the handle down to lock it.
3. Set the halogen oven to the appropriate wash function.
4. Turn the timer to the required time (usually around 10–15 minutes).

If your oven does not have this function, it is important to note that you should never immerse the lid in water (or any other liquids). The glass bowl can be placed in your dishwasher or washed as normal and the lid can be cleaned using a damp cloth.

Other equipment

In addition to your halogen oven, you may also need the following general kitchen equipment:

- Medium-size casserole dish
- Aluminium foil
- Small round baking/pizza tray
- Sieve
- Frying pan
- Grater
- Frying tray
- Measuring spoons and jugs
- Baking parchment
- Temperature gauge/thermometer
- Saucepan (various sizes)
- Mixing bowl (various sizes)
- Oven gloves
- Cling film
- Sharp knife
- Metal/bamboo skewers

It is also possible to purchase the following equipment, which is specifically for the halogen oven, from many halogen oven retailers:

- Steamer pan
- Frying pan
- Lid stand

Which food?

You can cook almost any food in your halogen oven, however, certain foods are more suitable. The following food can be cooked in your halogen oven:

- Meat/fish/poultry
- Vegetables
- Pizza
- Bread/cakes/pastry

Food can be cooked directly in the bowl or you can use the racks provided. It is worth noting, however, that the oven works by allowing air to circulate around the food so placing food directly in the bowl may mean increased cooking times. It is also possible to use a casserole dish or baking tray, just as you would in a conventional oven.

Don't forget that many ovens also have the ability to cook frozen food, and some even have thaw functions. However, remember that frozen food will take longer to cook but will still be quicker than in a conventional oven.

Vegetables

It's essential to remember that vegetables will generally take longer to cook than meat, so you will often need to start cooking them first, particularly root vegetables such as carrots and potatoes. You can cook them directly on the racks or in a casserole dish with a little water or oil.

Cooking times

Most halogen ovens have a lowest temperature setting of around 125°C (257°F) and a highest setting of 250°C (482°F). You will probably notice how similar these settings are to a conventional oven. However, the distinctive design of the halogen oven means that cooking times at the same temperature are vastly reduced.

General advice

- The glass lid gets very hot so avoid touching the lid without wearing oven gloves.
- Always check that the meat is fully cooked before serving.
- The ovens have a tendency to brown meat quite quickly on the outside.

- Use aluminium foil to avoid burning food and then remove for the last 5 minutes of the cooking time.
- Keep the halogen oven clean and clean the lid with a damp cloth regularly.

About the recipes

These recipes have been designed for use with the halogen oven and require a basic skill level. Some of the recipes also provide variations on the type of ingredients that can be used. It is advisable to familiarize yourself with the oven prior to use and to ensure that you have any additional equipment needed.

Chicken

Marinated chicken
with spiced yogurt

Serves 4

Preparation time 20 minutes, plus marinating

Cooking time 1 hour

1.5 kg (3 lb) oven-ready chicken, skin removed

450 ml (¾ pint) natural yogurt

2 garlic cloves, crushed

5 cm (2 inch) piece of fresh root ginger, finely chopped

2 dried chillies, crushed

½ teaspoon ground turmeric

1 teaspoon salt

½ teaspoon ground mixed spice

2 tablespoons chopped mint

1 tablespoon ground cumin

2 teaspoons caster sugar

pepper

To serve

basmati rice

herb salad

1 Put the chicken in a large bowl. In a separate bowl mix together 300 ml (½ pint) of the yogurt and the garlic, ginger, chillies, turmeric, salt, mixed spice, mint, cumin and sugar. Tip the mixture over the chicken, making sure the whole chicken is coated in marinade. Cover loosely and chill for at least 8 hours or overnight.

2 Transfer the chicken to the lower rack of the halogen oven, tipping over any of the yogurt mixture left in the bowl.

3 Set the temperature to 200°C (392°F) and cook the chicken for 1 hour, turning it after 20 minutes cooking and again after a further 20 minutes. Check that the meat is cooked through by piercing the thickest area of the thigh with a knife or skewer; the juices should run clear. If necessary cook for a little longer. Leave the chicken to stand in a warm place while you finish the sauce.

4 Pour the juices from the halogen oven bowl into a serving jug and stir in the remaining yogurt. Check the seasoning and serve with the chicken, basmati rice and a herb salad.

Spanish stuffed chicken
with couscous

Serves 4–6
Preparation time 15 minutes
Cooking time 1 hour

325 g (11 oz) can or jar pimientos

3 tablespoons olive oil

1 small onion, finely chopped

25 g (1 oz) blanched almonds,
  finely chopped

8 pitted green olives, chopped

1 large tomato, skinned, deseeded
  and chopped

50 g (2 oz) breadcrumbs

1.5 kg (3 lb) oven-ready chicken

salt and pepper

couscous, to serve

1 Thoroughly drain the pimientos, pat them dry on kitchen paper and cut them into small pieces.

2 Melt 2 tablespoons of the oil in a frying pan on the hob and gently fry the onion for 5 minutes to soften. Remove from the heat and stir in the pimientos, almonds, olives, tomato, breadcrumbs and a little seasoning.

3 Put the chicken on a board and remove the wishbone. Pack the stuffing into the neck cavity, wrap the skin under the bird and secure with a metal skewer. Shape the remaining stuffing into small balls.

4 Place the chicken on the lower rack of the halogen oven and brush with the remaining oil. Season with salt and pepper and place the stuffing balls around the chicken.

5 Set the temperature to 200°C (392°F) and cook the chicken for 1 hour, turning it after 20 minutes cooking and again after a further 20 minutes. Check that the meat is cooked through by piercing the thickest area of the thigh with a knife or skewer; the juices should run clear. If necessary, cook the chicken for a little longer.

6 Leave the chicken to stand in a warm place for 15 minutes before carving. Serve with couscous.

Chicken
with crème fraîche and cider

Serves 4
Preparation time 25 minutes
Cooking time 1 hour

25 g (1 oz) dried mushrooms

4 chicken legs, skinned

2 teaspoons plain flour

3 tablespoons olive oil

1 bunch of spring onions, thinly sliced

300 ml (½ pint) dry cider

4 tablespoons single cream

2 dessert apples, cored and cut into quarters

salt and pepper

To serve
mashed potatoes
stir-fried cabbage

1 Put the mushrooms in a heatproof bowl, cover with 100 ml (3½ fl oz) boiling water and leave to soak while you prepare the chicken.

2 Make several deep cuts along the fleshy side of each chicken leg. Season the flour with salt and pepper and use the mixture to coat the chicken. Heat the oil in a frying pan on the hob and fry the spring onions for 1 minute until wilted. Transfer to a plate with a slotted spoon. Add the chicken portions to the pan and fry on all sides until lightly browned. Transfer to a casserole dish.

3 Add the soaked mushrooms and soaking liquid, cider and a little seasoning to the pan and bring to the boil. Add to the casserole dish and arrange the apple pieces on top.

4 Cover with foil and place on the lower rack of the halogen oven. Set the temperature to 200°C (392°F) and cook for 55 minutes or until the chicken is cooked through.

5 Remove from the oven, stir in the prepared spring onions and cream and check the seasoning. Serve with buttery mashed potatoes and stir-fried cabbage.

Simple chicken curry

Serves 4
Preparation time 15 minutes
Cooking time 35 minutes

2 tablespoons sunflower oil

500 g (1 lb) diced chicken thighs

2 onions, thinly sliced

2 garlic cloves, crushed

1 tablespoon medium curry paste

2 tablespoons tomato purée

75 g (3 oz) creamed coconut, grated

2 bay leaves

1 tablespoon lemon juice

450 ml (¾ pint) chicken or
   vegetable stock

300 g (10 oz) waxy potatoes, diced

salt

coriander sprigs, to garnish

To serve
naan bread or chapattis
spinach (optional)

1 Heat the oil in a frying pan on the hob and gently fry the chicken, stirring, until pale golden. Stir in the onions and fry for a further 5 minutes. Add the garlic and curry paste and fry for a further 1 minute.

2 Stir in the tomato purée, coconut, bay leaves, lemon juice, stock and potatoes and bring just to the boil. Transfer to a casserole dish and cover with foil.

3 Place on the lower rack of the halogen oven. Set the temperature to 200°C (392°F) and cook for 25 minutes or until the chicken is cooked through. Garnish with coriander sprigs and serve with warm naan bread or chapattis and wilted spinach, if liked.

Chicken and chorizo burgers

Serves 4
Preparation time 15 minutes,
** plus chilling**
Cooking time 12 minutes

200 g (7 oz) natural cottage cheese
50 g (2 oz) chorizo sausage, diced
½ onion, roughly chopped
225 g (7½ oz) minced chicken
1 tablespoon chopped oregano
salt and pepper

To serve
burger buns
green salad
spicy relish

1 Put the cottage cheese in a metal sieve over a large bowl and press the mixture through the sieve with the back of a spoon.

2 Put the chorizo and onion in a food processor or blender and blend until finely chopped. Add the chicken, oregano and seasoning and blend until mixed. Tip the mixture into the cheese and mix well together (this is most easily done with your hands) until evenly combined.

3 Divide the mixture into 4 equal pieces and shape each into a burger. Chill for at least 1 hour.

4 Place the burgers in a lightly oiled tin on the upper rack of the halogen oven. Set the temperature to 200°C (392°F) and cook the burgers for 12 minutes, turning them over after 6 minutes, until cooked through. Serve in burger buns with a leafy green salad and spicy relish.

Chicken in red wine

Serves 4
Preparation time 25 minutes
Cooking time 1 hour

50 g (2 oz) butter

2 tablespoons olive oil

4 chicken drumsticks

4 chicken thighs

100 g (3½ oz) small shallots, peeled
and left whole

50 g (2 oz) smoked streaky bacon,
diced

2 carrots, diced

1 celery stick, diced

1 tablespoon plain flour

150 ml (¼ pint) chicken stock

300 ml (½ pint) red wine

3 tablespoons sun-dried tomato paste

3 garlic cloves, crushed

3 bay leaves

2 thick slices of white bread

salt and pepper

chopped parsley, to garnish

To serve
mashed potatoes
minted peas

1 Melt half the butter and oil in a frying pan on the hob and lightly brown the chicken on all sides. Transfer the chicken to a casserole dish.

2 Add the shallots, bacon, carrots and celery to the frying pan and cook gently for 6–8 minutes until beginning to brown. Sprinkle in the flour, stirring to mix. Gradually blend in the stock, wine and tomato paste. Add the garlic, bay leaves and a little seasoning. Bring to the boil and pour the mixture over the chicken. Cover with foil and place on the lower rack of the halogen oven.

3 Set the temperature to 200°C (392°F) and cook for 50–55 minutes or until the chicken is cooked through.

4 Meanwhile, remove the crusts from the bread and cut the rest of the bread into small cubes. Heat the remaining butter and oil in the cleaned frying pan and fry the bread, stirring, until lightly browned.

5 Remove the chicken from the oven and check the seasoning of the sauce. Serve with a scattering of croutons, creamy mashed potatoes and minted peas

Chicken goujons
with oven chips and tartare sauce

Serves 4
Preparation time 25 minutes
Cooking time 45 minutes

75 g (3 oz) breadcrumbs

3 tablespoons grated Parmesan
cheese

1 tablespoon chopped oregano
or parsley

1 egg

4 skinless chicken breasts

500 g (1 lb) medium potatoes

1 tablespoon sunflower oil

150 ml (¼ pint) mayonnaise

40 g (1½ oz) gherkins, finely
chopped

1 garlic clove, crushed

1 tablespoon capers, drained and
finely chopped

2 tablespoons chopped chives

salt and pepper

green salad, to serve (optional)

1 Mix the breadcrumbs with the Parmesan, oregano or parsley and a little seasoning. Tip the mixture on to a plate. Beat the egg on a separate plate.

2 Cut the chicken breasts into 1 cm (½ inch) strips. Coat the chicken pieces in the egg, then the breadcrumbs and space them slightly apart in an oiled, shallow tin. Place on the lower rack of the halogen oven. Set the temperature to 200°C (392°F) and cook for 20 minutes, turning once, until golden.

3 Cut the potatoes into chunky chips and toss them in a bowl with the oil and plenty of seasoning. Scatter in a lightly oiled, shallow tin on the upper rack of the oven. Cook for a further 25 minutes, turning the chips once or twice, until crisp and golden.

4 Meanwhile, mix together the mayonnaise, gherkins, garlic, capers, chives and a little seasoning and turn into a small serving bowl. Serve with the chicken, chips and a green salad, if liked.

Sticky glazed chicken drumsticks

Serves 4

Preparation time 10 minutes, plus marinating

Cooking time 25 minutes

4 tablespoons red wine vinegar

2 tablespoons dark soy sauce

2 tablespoons tomato purée

2 garlic cloves, crushed

generous pinch of cayenne pepper

1 tablespoon Worcestershire sauce

2 tablespoons clear honey

8 large chicken drumsticks, skinned

To serve

corn on the cob

watercress salad

1 In a small bowl mix together the vinegar, soy sauce, tomato purée, garlic, cayenne pepper, Worcestershire sauce and honey.

2 Make several deep cuts into the fleshy side of each drumstick. Place them in a shallow dish and add the sauce, turning the chicken until it is well coated. Cover loosely with clingfilm and chill for at least 2 hours or overnight.

3 Put a sheet of foil on the upper rack of the halogen oven, turning the edges up so that the juices will be contained as the chicken cooks. Brush the foil lightly with oil. Arrange the chicken on the foil and spoon over the marinade.

4 Set the temperature to 200°C (392°F) and cook for 25 minutes, turning the chicken occasionally and brushing with the marinade until cooked through. Serve with buttered corn on the cob and a watercress salad.

Beef

Rich beef stew
with tapenade

Serves 4
Preparation time 20 minutes
Cooking time 1½ hours

1 tablespoon plain flour

750 g (1½ lb) braising beef, cut into small pieces

3 tablespoons olive oil

1 large onion, chopped

3 carrots, sliced

4 garlic cloves, crushed

several pared strips of orange rind

several thyme sprigs

300 ml (½ pint) red wine

400 g (13 oz) can chopped tomatoes

4 tablespoons sun-dried tomato paste

1 tablespoon molasses or black treacle

5 tablespoons black olive tapenade

salt and pepper

polenta or pasta, to serve

1 Season the flour with salt and pepper and use it to coat the beef. Heat the oil in a frying pan on the hob and fry the meat, in batches, to brown, transferring the browned meat to a casserole dish. Add the onion and carrots to the pan and fry for 5 minutes to soften. Add the garlic and fry for a further 1 minute.

2 Add the orange rind, thyme, wine, tomatoes, tomato paste, molasses or treacle and a little seasoning to the pan and bring to the boil. Add the mixture to the casserole dish. Cover with foil and place the dish on the lower rack of the halogen oven.

3 Set the temperature to 175°C (347°F) and cook for 1¼ hours or until the beef is tender. Stir in the tapenade and cook for a further 10 minutes. Check the seasoning and serve with creamy polenta or pasta.

Slow cooked beef ribs

Serves 4–5
Preparation time 20 minutes
Cooking time about 2 hours

2 tablespoons plain flour

1.5 kg (3 lb) beef short ribs

3 tablespoons vegetable oil

1 large onion, chopped

4 carrots, sliced

2 celery sticks, sliced

3 tablespoons tomato purée

300 ml (½ pint) Guinness or beer

300 ml (½ pint) beef stock

3 tablespoons Worcestershire
   sauce

3 bay leaves

salt and pepper

chopped parsley, to garnish

To serve
mashed potatoes
seasonal vegetables

1 Season the flour with salt and pepper and use it to coat the meat. Heat the oil in a large frying pan on the hob and fry the ribs, in batches, to brown. Transfer to the base of the halogen oven. Add the onion, carrots and celery to the pan and fry for 5 minutes. Place on top of the meat.

2 Add the tomato purée, Guinness or beer, stock, Worcestershire sauce, bay leaves and a little seasoning to the pan and bring to the boil. Pour the mixture over the ribs.

3 Set the temperature to 150°C (302°F) and cook for about 2 hours or until very tender, turning the ribs occasionally. Check the seasoning and serve accompanied with mashed potatoes, seasonal vegetables and parsley sprinkled over the top.

Traditional beef satay

Serves 4

Preparation time 25 minutes, plus marinating

Cooking time 25 minutes

½ bunch of spring onions, chopped

2.5 cm (1 inch) piece of fresh root ginger, chopped

2 garlic cloves, chopped

8 cardamom pods

1 teaspoon each cumin and coriander seeds, lightly crushed

4 tablespoons lemon juice

½ teaspoon freshly grated nutmeg

2 bay leaves, crumbled

2 tablespoons vegetable oil

700 g (1 lb 7 oz) rump steak, trimmed and cut into chunks

6 tablespoons peanut butter

1 tablespoon light muscovado sugar

1 red chilli, deseeded and chopped

2 tablespoons dark soy sauce

150 ml (¼ pint) beef stock

To serve

rice

lime quarters

1 Put the spring onions, ginger, garlic, cardamom pods, cumin and coriander seeds, 2 tablespoons of the lemon juice, nutmeg, bay leaves and oil in a food processor or blender and blend to a paste.

2 Put the steak in a bowl, add the paste and stir well. Cover loosely and leave to marinate for at least 4 hours or overnight. Meanwhile, soak 8 wooden skewers in water.

3 Put the peanut butter, sugar, chilli, soy sauce, stock and the remaining lemon juice in a small saucepan and heat gently until the mixture has thickened.

4 Thread the meat on to the skewers and arrange them on a foil-lined baking sheet or shallow tin. (You will need to cook the beef skewers in batches.) Place the beef on the upper rack of the halogen oven.

5 Set the temperature to 200°C (392°F) and cook 4 of the beef skewers for 8–10 minutes, turning halfway through cooking, until golden. Transfer to a warm serving dish while you cook the remainder. Check the sauce for seasoning and serve with the beef, steamed rice and lime quarters.

Roast sirloin of beef

Serves 4–5
Preparation time 15 minutes
Cooking time 50 minutes

1.25 kg (2½ lb) piece of rolled
  sirloin of beef
2 large onions, sliced
several thyme sprigs
2 tablespoons olive oil
2 teaspoons plain flour
2 teaspoons dry mustard
200 ml (7 fl oz) red wine
salt and pepper

1 Rub the beef on all sides with plenty of salt and pepper. Scatter the onions and thyme sprigs in a roasting tin and rest the beef on top. Drizzle with the oil and place on the lower rack of the halogen oven.

2 Set the temperature to 225°C (437°F) and cook for 20 minutes, turning twice during cooking. Mix together the flour and mustard powder. Turn the meat so that the fat side is uppermost and sprinkle with the flour mixture. Cook for a further 15 minutes. (The beef will still be pink in the centre, so cook for a little longer if you prefer beef cooked through.) Transfer the meat to a board or platter and leave to rest for 20 minutes before carving.

3 Skim any fat from the juices in the roasting tin and fry the onions for 10 minutes. Pour in the wine and cook for a further 5 minutes. Season to taste and strain into a gravy jug. Serve with the beef.

Red pepper burgers

Serves 4–6

Preparation time 15 minutes, plus chilling

Cooking time 10–11 minutes

450 g (14½ oz) lean beef mince

1 small onion, finely grated

1 garlic clove, crushed

1 small red pepper, cored, deseeded and finely diced

½ teaspoon dried mixed herbs

2 tablespoons sweet chilli sauce

25–50 g (1–2 oz) fresh breadcrumbs

1 egg, beaten

1 tablespoon sunflower or vegetable oil

salt and pepper

To serve

burger buns

salad leaves

tomato slices

red onion slices

mayonnaise

1 In a large bowl mix together the beef, onion, garlic, red pepper, herbs, sweet chilli sauce and breadcrumbs. Season to taste with salt and pepper and mix in the egg. Combine thoroughly, cover and refrigerate for 30 minutes.

2 Divide the mixture into 4–6 equal pieces and shape into burgers. Brush each burger with oil and cook on the upper rack of the halogen oven at 200°C (392°F) for 10–11 minutes.

3 Serve the burgers in the split buns with salad leaves, slices of tomato and red onion and mayonnaise.

Classic steak and kidney pies

Serves 4

Preparation time 20 minutes

Cooking time about 1½–1¾ hours

1 tablespoon sunflower oil

450 g (14½ oz) lean braising or stewing steak, cubed

1 onion, sliced

100 g (3½ oz) chestnut mushrooms, quartered

225 g (7½ oz) ox kidney, cored, trimmed and cut into small pieces

1 tablespoon plain flour

450 ml (¾ pint) hot beef stock

200 ml (7 fl oz) ale

500 g (1 lb) shortcrust pastry (thawed if frozen)

1 egg, beaten

salt and pepper

To serve

peas

Chunky chips (see page 140)

1 Heat the oil in a large frying pan on the hob and cook the beef over a medium heat for 3–4 minutes until brown on all sides.

2 Add the onion and mushrooms to the pan and cook for a further 4–5 minutes until coloured. Add the kidneys and cook for 1–2 minutes. Sprinkle over the flour.

3 Transfer the meat and vegetables to a casserole dish and add the stock and ale. Season to taste with salt and pepper. Put the casserole on the lower rack of the halogen oven, cover with foil and cook at 200°C (392°F) for 45–50 minutes or until the meat is tender. Spoon the cooked mixture into 2 individual pie dishes.

4 Roll out the pastry and cut out 2 lids slightly larger than each dish. Place the pastry lid on top of the meat filling, dampening the edges of each dish. Trim away the excess pastry and press the edges to seal. Brush the tops with egg and cook the pies at 225°C (437°F) for 20–25 minutes or until the pastry is golden, covering the pastry for the first 10–15 minutes so that it does not burn.

5 Cut the pies in half and serve with garden peas and chunky chips.

Grilled steak
with sorrel cream sauce

Serves 4
Preparation time 10 minutes
Cooking time 15 minutes

4 fillet steaks, each 175 g (6 oz)
1 garlic clove, skinned and crushed
50 g (2 oz) butter
2 shallots, finely chopped
150 ml (¼ pint) single cream
75 g (3 oz) sorrel, shredded
salt and pepper
Chunky chips (see page 140),
  to serve

1 Rub the steaks with the garlic and a little seasoning and place them on the upper rack of the halogen oven.

2 Set the temperature to 250°C (482°F) and cook for 3 minutes on each side. (Cook for a little longer if you prefer your steaks well done.) Remove from the oven and keep warm while you make the sauce.

3 Remove the rack from the oven and add the butter to the halogen oven bowl. Cook briefly at 200°C (392°F) until melted. Add the shallots and cook for 3 minutes. Stir in the cream and sorrel and cook for 5 minutes until heated through. Season to taste and spoon over the steaks. Serve with Chunky chips.

Chilli spiced meatballs

Serves 4
Preparation time 25 minutes
Cooking time 15–20 minutes

1 large onion, roughly chopped
1 red chilli, deseeded and chopped
2 garlic cloves, chopped
1 teaspoon shrimp paste
2 teaspoons coriander seeds
2 teaspoons cumin seeds
450 g (14½ oz) lean minced beef
2 teaspoons dark soy sauce
1 teaspoon dark muscovado sugar
juice of ½ lemon
1 egg, beaten
a little oil for brushing
salt and pepper
sliced spring onions, to garnish

To serve
noodles
sweet dipping sauce

1 Put the onion, chilli, garlic and shrimp paste in a food processor or blender and blend to a paste. (Don't over mix or the onion will become too wet.)

2 In a small frying pan on the hob heat the coriander and cumin seeds until they start to release their aroma. Put the beef in a mixing bowl and add the onion mixture, coriander and cumin seeds, soy sauce, sugar and lemon juice. Add the egg and mix until evenly combined. (This is most easily done with your hands.)

3 Shape the mixture into balls, each about the size of a golf ball. Lightly oil a shallow ovenproof tin or dish, add the meatballs and place on the upper rack of the halogen oven.

4 Set the temperature to 200°C (392°F) and cook the meatballs for 15–20 minutes or until cooked through. Garnish with sliced spring onions and serve with noodles and a sweet dipping sauce.

Lamb

Lamb chops
with ginger and orange

Serves 4
Preparation time 15 minutes
Cooking time 50 minutes

4 large chump chops

2 tablespoons vegetable oil

1 large onion, finely chopped

1 whole orange, plus the finely
grated rind of 1 orange and
2 tablespoons juice

2 tablespoons sun-dried tomato
paste

1 tablespoon light muscovado
sugar

15 g (½ oz) fresh root ginger, grated

300 ml (½ pint) hot lamb or
chicken stock

2 teaspoons cornflour

salt and pepper

To serve
basmati rice
watercress salad

1 Season the chops on both sides with
salt and pepper. Heat 1 tablespoon of
the oil in a frying pan on the hob and fry
the chops until lightly browned on both
sides. Transfer to a casserole dish.

2 Add the onion to the frying pan and
fry gently for about 5 minutes until
softened. Add to the dish.

3 Mix together the orange rind and
juice, tomato paste, sugar, ginger and
stock in a jug. Add a little seasoning and
pour the mixture over the chops. Cover
with foil and place on the lower rack of
the halogen oven.

4 Set the temperature to 200°C (392°F)
and cook for about 30 minutes or
until the meat is tender. Remove the
chops from the dish.

5 Blend the cornflour with
2 tablespoons water and stir into the
casserole juices. Return the lamb to the
dish and cook, uncovered, for a further
5–10 minutes or until the juices have
thickened slightly.

6 Meanwhile, cut the whole orange in
half widthways, then into quarters.
Heat the remaining oil in the frying
pan and lightly sear the orange pieces
on the cut sides. Serve with the lamb,
accompanied by basmati rice and a
watercress salad.

Summer roast lamb

Serves 4

Preparation time 15 minutes, plus marinating

Cooking time 55 minutes

2 tablespoons olive oil

3 tablespoons red wine

2 teaspoons ground cumin

2 teaspoons hot paprika

1 teaspoon coarsely ground black pepper

1.5 kg (3 lb) leg of lamb

2 garlic cloves, thinly sliced

salt

To serve

Greek salad

pitta bread

1 In a small bowl mix together the oil, wine, cumin, paprika and black pepper.

2 Place the lamb in a shallow dish and make small slits over the surface. Push a slice of garlic into each slit. Spoon over the spice mixture and spread it all over the lamb. Cover loosely with clingfilm and leave to marinate for several hours, occasionally spooning the marinade over the meat. Place the lamb on the lower rack of the halogen oven.

3 Set the temperature to 250°C (482°F) and cook the lamb for 15 minutes. Reduce the temperature to 200°C (392°F) and cook for a further 40 minutes, spreading over any remaining marinade in the dish during cooking. (The lamb will be slightly pink in the centre, so cook it for a little longer if you prefer it well done.)

4 Transfer the lamb to a carving platter or board and leave to rest for about 20 minutes before carving. Serve with a Greek salad and warm pitta bread.

Lamb and tomato couscous

Serves 6

Preparation time 20 minutes

Cooking time 1 hour

450 g (14½ oz) lamb tenderloin, cut into small pieces

3 tablespoons olive oil

2 onions, sliced

4 small carrots, sliced

1 green pepper, cored, deseeded and cut into small pieces

2 garlic cloves, crushed

400 g (13 oz) can chopped tomatoes

2 teaspoons light muscovado sugar

1 teaspoon each of ground turmeric, coriander, cumin and chilli powder

100 g (3½ oz) pitted dates, chopped

300 g (10 oz) couscous

2 teaspoons vegetable stock bouillon powder

salt and pepper

1 Season the lamb with salt and pepper. Heat the oil in a frying pan on the hob and fry the lamb until browned. Transfer to a casserole dish.

2 Add the onions, carrots and green pepper to the pan and fry for 5 minutes to soften. Stir in the garlic, tomatoes, sugar, spices and a little seasoning and bring to the boil. Add to the casserole dish. Stir in the dates. Cover the dish with foil and place on the lower rack of the halogen oven.

3 Set the temperature to 200°C (392°F) and cook for 45 minutes or until the lamb is tender. Towards the end of the cooking time put the couscous and bouillon powder in a bowl and add 425 ml (15 fl oz) boiling water. Cover and leave to stand for 10 minutes until the water is absorbed. Fluff up the couscous with a fork and serve with the lamb.

Lamb
with spicy sausage

Serves 6
Preparation time 15 minutes
Cooking time 30–35 minutes

2 tablespoons plain flour

450 g (14½ oz) lean lamb, cut into
   2.5 cm (1 inch) cubes

2 tablespoons olive oil

100 g (3½ oz) chorizo or spicy
   paprika sausage, skinned and cut
   into large pieces

1 red onion, finely chopped

2 garlic cloves, crushed

300 ml (½ pint) hot lamb stock

150 ml (¼ pint) red wine

410 g (13¼ oz) can black-eye peas
   or butter beans, rinsed and
   drained

salt and pepper

Spicy sweet potatoes (see
   page 130), to serve

1 Season the flour with salt and pepper and coat the lamb in the mixture.

2 Heat the oil in a large, nonstick frying pan and cook the lamb and chorizo over a medium heat for 3–4 minutes or until brown. Transfer to a large, ovenproof casserole dish. (You will need a casserole that holds about 3 litres (5¼ pints), but check first that it will fit inside your halogen oven.)

3 In the same frying pan fry the onion and garlic for about 5 minutes until soft. Transfer to the casserole together with the stock and wine and place on the lower rack of the halogen oven.

4 Set the temperature to 200°C (392°F) and cook for 22–25 minutes, stirring occasionally. About 10 minutes before the end of the cooking time add the beans and reduce the temperature to 150°C (302°F).

5 Serve the lamb with Spicy sweet potatoes.

Lamb ragout

Serves 6
Preparation time 20 minutes
Cooking time 30–37 minutes

1 tablespoon olive oil

675 g (1 lb 6 oz) boneless lamb
 shoulder, leg or neck fillet, cut
 into 2.5 cm (1 inch) cubes

grated rind of 1 lemon

2 garlic cloves, crushed

6 spring onions, finely chopped

150 ml (¼ pint) cider or white
 wine

600 ml (1 pint) hot lamb or
 vegetable stock

2 bay leaves

100 g (3½ oz) sweet corn kernels

75 g (3 oz) cauliflower florets

2 courgettes, roughly chopped

75 g (3 oz) sugar snap peas

small handful of chopped mint
 leaves

salt and pepper

new potatoes, to serve

1 Heat the oil in a large ovenproof casserole dish, add the lamb, lemon rind and garlic and cook on the hob, stirring occasionally, over a medium heat for 4–5 minutes until brown. Transfer to a plate.

2 Add the spring onions to the casserole dish and cook for 1–2 minutes until soft. Return the lamb to the casserole and add the cider or wine, hot stock and bay leaves. Transfer the casserole to the lower rack of the halogen oven.

3 Set the temperature to 200°C (392°F) and cook for 20 minutes. Add the sweet corn, cauliflower and courgettes and cook for a further 5–10 minutes.

4 Season to taste with salt and pepper, stir through the sugar snap peas and mint and serve immediately with new potatoes.

Easy lamb curry

Serves 2
Preparation time 10 minutes
Cooking time 30 minutes

25 g (1 oz) butter

2 tablespoons vegetable oil

350 g (11½ oz) lean lamb, diced

1 onion, sliced

2 garlic cloves, chopped

1 cinnamon stick, halved

6 cardamom pods, crushed to open

1 teaspoon each of ground cumin,
ginger and chilli powder

2 teaspoons garam masala

salt

chopped coriander, to garnish

basmati rice, to serve

1 Melt the butter with the oil in a frying pan on the hob and fry the lamb until browned. Transfer to a casserole dish.

2 Add the onion to the pan and fry gently for 5 minutes. Stir in the garlic and spices and fry for a further 2 minutes. Stir in 250 ml (8 fl oz) water and bring just to the boil. Pour over the lamb. Place on the lower rack of the halogen oven.

3 Set the temperature to 200°C (392°F) and cook for 20 minutes until the lamb is tender, stirring twice. Garnish with chopped coriander and serve with basmati rice.

Lamb hotpot

Serves 2
Preparation time 15 minutes
Cooking time about 1 hour

4 lean lamb chops
25 g (1 oz) butter
1 onion, thinly sliced
1 teaspoon chopped rosemary
1 garlic clove, crushed
2 medium potatoes, thinly sliced
200 ml (7 fl oz) hot lamb or chicken
    stock
salt and pepper
green vegetables, to serve

1 Trim any excess fat from the lamb and season lightly on both sides with salt and pepper.

2 Reserve a little piece of the butter and melt the remainder in a frying pan on the hob and fry the chops until lightly brown. Transfer to a shallow casserole dish. Add the onion, rosemary and garlic to the frying pan and fry for 3 minutes. Scatter on top of the lamb.

3 Layer the potatoes on top and pour over the stock. Dot with the reserved butter, season lightly and cover with foil. Place the dish on the lower rack of the halogen oven.

4 Set the temperature to 200°C (392°F) and cook for 30–40 minutes until the potatoes are tender. Remove the foil and cook for a further 10 minutes until the surface is golden. Serve with seasonal green vegetables.

Lamb tikka kebabs
with cucumber salad

Serves 4

**Preparation time 20 minutes,
 plus marinating**

Cooking time 20 minutes

150 ml (¼ pint) natural yogurt

1 garlic clove, crushed

1 teaspoon ground coriander

juice of ½ lemon

1 tablespoon chopped parsley

½ teaspoon ground turmeric

1 teaspoon chilli powder

1 teaspoon garam masala

450 g (14½ oz) lamb tenderloin,
  cut into 2.5 cm (1 inch) pieces

coriander sprigs, to garnish

Cucumber salad

1 cucumber

1 garlic clove, crushed

1 tablespoon chopped mint

1 teaspoon caster sugar

150 ml (¼ pint) natural yogurt

To serve

naan bread

lime quarters

1 In a large bowl mix together the yogurt, garlic, coriander, lemon juice, parsley, turmeric, chilli powder and garam masala. Add the lamb and stir to mix. Cover loosely and refrigerate for at least 4 hours or overnight. Meanwhile, soak 8 wooden skewers in cold water.

2 Thread the lamb on to the skewers and place them on the upper rack of the halogen oven.

3 Set the temperature to 225°C (437°F) and cook the kebabs for about 20 minutes, turning them a couple of times so they cook evenly.

4 Meanwhile, make the salad. Peel and halve the cucumber and discard the seeds. Dice the flesh and mix it in a bowl with the garlic, mint, sugar and yogurt.

5 Garnish the kebabs with coriander sprigs and serve with the salad, warm naan bread and lime quarters.

Pork

Pesto pork
with tomatoes

Serves 4
Preparation time 25 minutes
Cooking time 40 minutes

2 tablespoons olive oil

1 small onion, finely chopped

4 tablespoons sun-dried tomato
  pesto

1 teaspoon dried oregano

25 g (1 oz) breadcrumbs

4 pieces of pork tenderloin, each
  150 g (5 oz)

15 g (½ oz) butter

2 teaspoons plain flour

300 ml (½ pint) dry white wine

8 pitted green olives, roughly
  sliced

100 g (3½ oz) cherry tomatoes,
  halved

finely grated rind of 1 lemon

2 tablespoons chopped parsley

salt and pepper

pasta, to serve

1 Heat 1 tablespoon of the oil in a small frying pan on the hob and gently fry the onion for 5 minutes. Remove from the heat and stir in the pesto, oregano, breadcrumbs and a little seasoning. Leave to cool.

2 Make a horizontal cut through each piece of pork so that the meat is almost sliced in half. Open out the pieces and place them between sheets of baking parchment. Beat them with a rolling pin or meat mallet to flatten slightly.

3 Spread the tomato mixture evenly over the pork and fold the pieces back in half. Secure with string at 3 cm (1¼ inch) intervals. Heat the remaining oil in the frying pan and lightly brown the pork on all sides. Transfer to a shallow ovenproof dish.

4 Melt the butter in the frying pan, add the flour and stir over a gentle heat for 30 seconds. Gradually blend in the wine and bring to the boil. Pour the mixture over the pork, cover the dish with foil and place on the lower rack of the halogen oven.

5 Set the temperature to 200°C (392°F) and cook for 25 minutes. Add the olives and cherry tomatoes to the dish and cook, uncovered, for a further 5 minutes or until the meat is cooked through. Check the seasoning and sprinkle with chopped parsley. Serve with fresh ribbon pasta.

Spicy glazed pork kebabs

Serves 4

Preparation time 15 minutes, plus marinating

Cooking time 15 minutes

5 tablespoons mango chutney

2 tablespoons white wine vinegar

2 tablespoons Worcestershire sauce

1 teaspoon Dijon mustard

1 garlic clove, crushed

generous pinch of chilli powder

500 g (1 lb) lean pork tenderloin, cut into 2 cm (¾ inch) chunks

salt and pepper

To serve

pitta bread

cucumber and lettuce salad

1 Finely chop any large pieces in the chutney. Mix the chutney in a large bowl with the wine vinegar, Worcestershire sauce, mustard, garlic, chilli powder and a little seasoning. Stir in the pork and mix until coated in the marinade. Cover loosely and chill for at least 2 hours. Meanwhile, soak 8 wooden skewers in water.

2 Thread the pork on to the skewers and arrange them in a shallow ovenproof tin. Place on the upper rack of the halogen oven.

3 Set the temperature to 200°C (392°F) and cook the kebabs for about 15 minutes, turning occasionally so they cook evenly. Serve in warm pitta breads with a cucumber and lettuce salad.

Pork
with peppercorns and dill

Serves 6
Preparation time 15 minutes
Cooking time 50 minutes

1 tablespoon plain flour

6 pork chump chops or leg steaks

25 g (1 oz) butter

1 tablespoon vegetable oil

1 large onion, finely chopped

150 ml (¼ pint) chicken stock

2 tablespoons green peppercorns
   in brine, drained

4 tablespoons chopped dill

200 ml (7 fl oz) soured cream

salt and pepper

rice, to serve

1 Season the flour with salt and pepper and coat the pork in the mixture.

2 Melt the butter with the oil in a frying pan on the hob and fry the pork on both sides to brown. Transfer to a shallow ovenproof dish.

3 Add the onion to the frying pan and fry gently for 5 minutes. Stir in the stock and bring to the boil. Stir in the peppercorns and pour the mixture over the meat. Cover with foil and place on the lower rack of the halogen oven.

4 Set the temperature to 200°C (392°F) and cook for 40 minutes or until the meat is tender. Remove the meat from the dish and stir in the dill and soured cream. Return the meat and cook, uncovered, for a further 5 minutes. Check the seasoning and serve with steamed rice.

Sausage casserole

Serves 4
Preparation time 10 minutes
Cooking time 15–20 minutes

1 tablespoon oil

500 g (1 lb) new potatoes, halved

8 sausages

1 onion, chopped

1 green pepper, cored, deseeded and diced

350 g (11½ oz) ready-made tomato pasta sauce

1 Heat the oil in a frying pan on the hob, add the potatoes and sausages and cook over a medium heat for 5 minutes, turning the sausages from time to time so that they brown evenly. Add the onion and pepper and cook for a further 5 minutes.

2 Transfer the mixture to a casserole dish and stir in the pasta sauce. Put the casserole dish on the lower rack of the halogen oven and cover with foil.

3 Set the temperature to 200°C (392°F) and cook for 5–10 minutes. To serve spoon on to 4 warm serving plates.

Toad-in-the-hole

Serves 4
Preparation time 20 minutes
Cooking time 40–50 minutes

125 g (4 oz) plain white flour
1 teaspoon salt
3 eggs
175 ml (6 fl oz) milk
4 tablespoons vegetable oil
8 pork sausages

Onion gravy
2 teaspoons oil
250 g (8 oz) red onions, sliced
2 rounded teaspoons plain flour
450 ml (¾ pint) vegetable stock
1 teaspoon caster sugar
2 teaspoons Worcestershire sauce

1 Make the batter. Put the flour and salt in a large bowl, make a well in the centre and add the eggs. Mix in half the milk until the mixture is smooth, then add the remaining milk. Whisk until fully combined and the surface is covered with tiny bubbles. Set aside to rest.

2 Meanwhile, put the vegetable oil and sausages in a small roasting tin and put it on the lower rack of the halogen oven. Set the temperature to 200°C (392°F) and cook for 10–11 minutes or until the sausages are browned.

3 Make sure that the oil in the roasting tin is really hot and pour the batter over the sausages. Cook, still at 200°C (392°F), for 30–40 minutes or until the batter has risen and is golden brown.

4 Meanwhile, make the onion gravy. Heat the oil in a large frying pan on the hob and cook the onions over a medium heat for about 8 minutes.

5 Stir in the flour and cook for a further 1–2 minutes. Add a little of the stock at a time, stirring to make a smooth sauce, then add the sugar and Worcestershire sauce. Simmer for about 5 minutes.

6 Cut the toad-in-the-hole into 4 portions and serve with the onion gravy.

Loin of pork
with red cabbage

Serves 4

Preparation time 15 minutes

**Cooking time 1 hour 10
  minutes**

450 g (14½ oz) red cabbage, thinly
  shredded

1 kg (2 lb) boned pork loin, skin
  scored

1 teaspoon celery salt

25 g (1 oz) butter

2 small onions, thinly sliced

2 dessert apples, peeled, cored
  and sliced

2 tablespoons red wine vinegar

2 tablespoons dark muscovado
  sugar

4 whole star anise

salt and pepper

mashed potatoes, to serve

1 Bring a saucepan of water to the
boil. Add the cabbage and cook for
1 minute. Drain and rinse under cold
running water.

2 Remove the skin from the pork and
rub it with a little salt. Season the
pork with celery salt and pepper. Melt
the butter in a frying pan on the hob
and fry the pork on all sides to brown.
Remove from the pan.

3 Add the onions to the pan and fry
gently for 5 minutes. Stir in the
apples, vinegar, sugar, star anise and
cabbage and mix well. Turn the mixture
into a large ovenproof dish and rest the
pork on top, nestling it down into the
cabbage. Cover with foil and place on
the lower rack of the halogen oven.

4 Set the temperature to 200°C (392°F)
and cook for 30 minutes. Remove the
foil and rest the crackling on top of the
pork. Cook for a further 30 minutes until
the crackling is crisped and the pork is
cooked through.

5 Transfer the pork to a board or
serving platter, cover with foil and
leave to stand for 15 minutes before
carving. Separate the crackling into
pieces and serve with the pork, cabbage
and buttery mashed potatoes.

Chilli pork ribs

Serves 4–6

Preparation time 10 minutes, plus marinating

Cooking time 20 minutes

2 teaspoons chilli powder

6 tablespoons sunflower oil

1 teaspoon barbecue seasoning

finely grated rind and juice of
  1 lime

2 garlic cloves, crushed

3 tablespoons tomato ketchup

16–18 pork spare ribs

chopped chives, to garnish

To serve

jacket potatoes

green salad

1 In a small bowl mix together the chilli powder, oil, barbecue seasoning, lime rind and juice, garlic and tomato ketchup.

2 Place the ribs in a shallow dish and brush with the marinade. Cover loosely and chill for at least 2 hours.

3 Arrange the ribs on the upper rack of the halogen oven. Set the temperature to 200°C (392°F) and cook the ribs for about 20 minutes, turning them once, until golden. Serve with jacket potatoes and a green salad.

Pot roasted pork
with apples and cider

Serves 6
Preparation time 25 minutes
Cooking time 1¼ hours

1.5 kg (3 lb) boned and rolled leg of
pork

4 tablespoons vegetable oil

several rosemary sprigs

1.25 kg (2½ lb) potatoes, thickly
sliced

2 dessert apples, cored and thickly
sliced

175 ml (6 fl oz) dry cider

salt and pepper

seasonal vegetables, to serve

1 If not already scored, use a sharp
knife to score the skin of the pork at
1 cm (½ inch) intervals. Sprinkle with salt
and drizzle with 1 tablespoon of the oil.
Rub over the surface of the skin. Scatter
the rosemary into a roasting tin, place the
pork on top and put it on the lower rack
of the halogen oven.

2 Set the temperature to 200°C (392°F)
and cook for 45 minutes.

3 Meanwhile, cook the potatoes
in a large saucepan of boiling,
lightly salted water for 5 minutes until
beginning to soften. Drain thoroughly
and toss with the remaining oil.

4 Scatter the apples and onion around
the pork and pour over the cider.
Arrange the potatoes on top and season
to taste with salt and pepper.

5 Return to the oven and cook for a
further 30 minutes until the pork
is cooked through and the potatoes are
golden. Leave to rest for 20 minutes
before serving with seasonal vegetables.

Seafood

Halibut
with tomatoes and basil

Serves 4

Preparation time 20 minutes, plus marinating

Cooking time 35 minutes

2 tablespoons lemon juice

5 tablespoons olive oil

4 halibut steaks

3 shallots, sliced

1 head of fennel, thinly sliced

300 g (10 oz) tomatoes, skinned, deseeded and chopped

3 tablespoons sun-dried tomato paste

2 teaspoons caster sugar

300 ml (½ pint) dry white wine

1 teaspoon fennel seeds, crushed

handful of basil leaves, shredded

salt and pepper

basil leaves, to garnish

To serve

crusty bread

green salad (optional)

1 Mix together the lemon juice, 3 tablespoons of the oil and a little salt and pepper. Spoon the mixture over the halibut and leave to marinate for 1–2 hours.

2 Heat the remaining oil in a large frying pan on the hob and gently fry the shallots and fennel for about 10 minutes until they are soft but not browned. Stir in the tomatoes, tomato paste, sugar, wine, fennel seeds, basil and seasoning and bring to the boil. Turn the mixture into a shallow ovenproof dish and place the halibut on top. Cover with foil and place on the lower rack of the halogen oven.

3 Set the temperature to 250°C (482°F) and cook for about 25 minutes until the fish is cooked through. (Test by piercing with the tip of a knife; it should flake easily.) Check the seasoning and transfer to shallow bowls. Scatter with basil leaves and serve with warm crusty bread and a leafy green salad, if liked.

Quick and easy paella

Serves 4
Preparation time 10 minutes
Cooking time 40 minutes

4 tablespoons olive oil

1 onion, chopped

1 green pepper, cored, deseeded
  and diced

100 g (3½ oz) chorizo sausage, cut
  into small dice

2 garlic cloves, crushed

250 g (8 oz) paella rice

400 g (13 oz) can chopped tomatoes

500 ml (17 fl oz) chicken or fish
  stock

1 teaspoon saffron threads

100 g (3½ oz) peas

200 g (7 oz) cooked peeled prawns

300 g (10 oz) frozen cooked
  mussels, thawed

salt and pepper

lemon or lime wedges, to serve

1 Heat the oil in a frying pan on the hob and fry the onion, green pepper and chorizo for 5 minutes to soften. Add the garlic and cook for a further 2 minutes.

2 Sprinkle in the rice and cook, stirring, for 2 minutes. Stir in the tomatoes, stock and saffron and bring to the boil. Pour the mixture into an ovenproof dish, cover with foil and place on the lower rack of the halogen oven.

3 Set the temperature to 200°C (392°F) and cook for 20 minutes. Stir in the peas, prawns and mussels. Cover and cook for a further 10 minutes or until the rice is tender and the liquid has been absorbed, adding a little boiling water if the paella dries out before the rice is cooked. Check the seasoning and serve with lemon or lime wedges.

Grilled mustard mackerel

Serves 2
Preparation time 10 minutes
Cooking time 10 minutes

2 mackerel, heads removed

15 g (½ oz) butter, melted

4 teaspoons grainy mustard

finely grated rind of 1 lime, plus
  2 tablespoons juice

1 tablespoon white wine vinegar

2 tablespoons clear honey

1 small garlic clove, crushed

1 tablespoon chopped chives

salt

To serve
rocket salad

new potatoes

1 Use a sharp knife to score 3 deep cuts along either side of each mackerel. Brush a shallow ovenproof dish with a little of the butter. Place the mackerel in the dish and brush with the remainder. Put on the upper rack of the halogen oven.

2 Set the temperature to 200°C (392°F) and cook for 5 minutes.

3 Mix together the mustard, lime rind and juice, vinegar, honey, garlic and a little salt. Turn the fish over and spread with the mustard mixture. Cook for a further 5 minutes or until the fish is cooked through. (Test by piercing the thickest area with the tip of a sharp knife; the fish should flake easily.)

4 Sprinkle the chives over the fish and serve with a rocket salad and buttered new potatoes.

Cod fillet
with coriander cream sauce

Serves 4
Preparation time 5 minutes
Cooking time 15 minutes

2 teaspoons plain flour

2 teaspoons ground coriander

4 cod fillets, each 200 g (7 oz)

2 tablespoons olive oil

1 tablespoon lemon juice

1 tablespoon capers

1 egg yolk

100 ml (3½ fl oz) single cream

salt and pepper

chopped coriander, to garnish

To serve

new potatoes

green salad

1 Mix the flour with the ground coriander and a little seasoning on a plate. Use the mixture to coat the cod fillets.

2 Put the oil in a shallow ovenproof dish and place it on the upper rack of the halogen oven. Set the temperature to 250°C (482°F) and heat the oil for 3 minutes. Add the fish portions and cook for 3–4 minutes on each side until just cooked through. (Test by piercing the fish with the tip of a knife; it should flake easily.) Drizzle with the lemon juice and scatter over the capers. Cook for a further 2 minutes.

3 Remove the fish to warm serving plates. Mix together the egg yolk and cream and stir into the juices remaining in the dish. Heat through for 3–4 minutes, season to taste and spoon over the fish. Serve garnished with chopped coriander and accompanied with new potatoes and a green salad.

Honey and sesame salmon

Serves 2
Preparation time 10 minutes
Cooking time 10–12 minutes

1 tablespoon clear honey

1 tablespoon light soy sauce

2 plump salmon fillets, each about
  150 g (5 oz)

2 spring onions, finely chopped

2 tablespoons sesame seeds

To serve

new potatoes

rocket salad

1 In a small bowl mix together the honey and soy sauce.

2 Lightly oil a sheet of foil and arrange the salmon fillets side by side on it. Brush the fillets with the honey mixture and sprinkle first with the spring onions, then the sesame seeds. Place on the upper rack of the halogen oven.

3 Set the temperature to 225°C (437°F) and cook for 10–12 minutes until the salmon is cooked through. (Test by piercing the plumpest area of the flesh with a knife; the flesh should flake easily.) Serve with buttered new potatoes and a rocket salad.

Salmon fishcakes

Makes 12 fishcakes
Preparation time 15 minutes
Cooking time 18–22 minutes

750 g (1½ lb) potatoes, cut into
    large chunks

25–30 g (1–1¼ oz) butter

210 g (7½ oz) can red salmon,
    drained

2 tablespoons chopped parsley

1 egg, beaten

1 tablespoon flour

salt and pepper

To serve
lettuce leaves
lemon wedges

1 Cook the potatoes in a large saucepan of boiling, lightly salted water for 10–12 minutes or until they are tender. Drain and return to the pan.

2 Mash the potatoes with the butter and stir in the salmon and parsley. Season to taste with salt and pepper and mix with sufficient egg for the mixture to bind together. Divide the mixture into 12 equal portions and shape them into patties.

3 Lightly coat each fishcake with flour and arrange them on the lower rack of the halogen oven.

4 Set the temperature to 250°C (482°F) and cook for 8–10 minutes or until golden brown, covering them with foil for the first 5 minutes so that they don't burn.

5 Serve the fishcakes on a bed of crisp lettuce with lemon wedges to squeeze over.

Malaysian prawn curry

Serves 4
Preparation time 25 minutes
Cooking time 35 minutes

2 tablespoons vegetable oil

2 onions, sliced

3 cm (1¼ inch) piece of fresh root
ginger, finely chopped

2 garlic cloves, crushed

2 teaspoons cumin seeds, crushed

2 teaspoons coriander seeds,
crushed

1 teaspoon dried chilli flakes

1 cinnamon stick

500 ml (17 fl oz) fish stock

2 tablespoons lime juice

1 tablespoon caster sugar

2 tablespoons light soy sauce

1 green pepper, cored, deseeded
and diced

4 teaspoons cornflour

225 g (7½ oz) can pineapple slices
in natural juice, drained (reserve
the juice)

400 g (13 oz) raw peeled and
deveined prawns

salt

noodles or rice, to serve

1 Heat the oil in a large frying pan or wok on the hob and fry the onions for about 8 minutes until they begin to brown. Stir in the ginger, garlic, cumin and coriander seeds, chilli flakes and cinnamon and cook for a further 2 minutes.

2 Pour in the stock and add the lime juice, sugar, soy sauce and green pepper and bring almost to the boil. Pour the mixture into an ovenproof casserole dish and cover with foil. Place on the lower rack of the halogen oven.

3 Set the temperature to 225°C (437°F) and cook for 15 minutes.

4 Meanwhile, blend the cornflour with 4 tablespoons of the reserved pineapple juice in a small bowl. Chop the pineapple pieces and add them to the casserole along with the cornflour paste and the prawns. Cook, uncovered, for a further 10 minutes or until the sauce has thickened and the prawns are pink and cooked through. Serve with sesame noodles or steamed rice.

Family fish pie

Serves 4
Preparation time 30 minutes
Cooking time 45–50 minutes

1 kg (2 lb) floury potatoes

625 g (1¼ lb) cod, pollack or haddock fillet, skinned

600 ml (1 pint) milk

100 g (3½ oz) butter

1 onion, finely chopped

2 celery sticks, thinly sliced

2 tablespoons chopped parsley

40 g (1½ oz) plain flour

100 g (3½ oz) mature Cheddar cheese, grated

100 ml (3½ fl oz) single cream or milk

salt and pepper

1 Cook the potatoes in a large saucepan of boiling, lightly salted water for 20 minutes or until tender. Drain and return to the pan. Set aside.

2 Meanwhile, put the fish in a shallow ovenproof dish with half the milk and place on the lower rack of the halogen oven.

3 Set the temperature to 250°C (482°F) and cook for 20 minutes until the fish is cooked through. Pour off the milk, reserving it for the sauce, and flake the fish evenly over the bottom of the dish.

4 Melt 25 g (1 oz) of the butter in a saucepan and gently fry the onion and celery for about 5 minutes until softened. Spoon the onion–celery mixture over the flaked fish and scatter over the parsley.

5 Make the sauce. Melt a further 50 g (2 oz) of the butter in a clean saucepan and stir in the flour to make a smooth paste. Remove from the heat and gradually blend in all the reserved milk. Return to the heat and bring to the boil, stirring continuously, until thickened. Stir in half the cheese and season to taste with salt and pepper. Spoon the sauce over the fish.

6 Mash the potatoes with the cream and remaining butter and season to taste. Add the potatoes to the dish, spreading them in an even layer over the fish. Scatter the remaining cheese over the potatoes and place on the lower rack of the halogen oven.

7 Set the temperature to 200°C (392°F) and cook for 20–25 minutes until the surface is golden. Cover the pie with foil if the topping becomes too brown.

Vegetarian

Vegetable stew
with herb dumplings

Serves 4
Preparation time 20 minutes
Cooking time about 1 hour

25 g (1 oz) butter

1 onion, chopped

1 leek, thickly sliced

3 carrots, roughly chopped

2 celery sticks, roughly chopped

2 garlic cloves, crushed

2 tablespoons plain flour

1 litre (1¾ pints) vegetable stock

4 tablespoons sun-dried tomato
  pesto

400 g (13 oz) can haricot beans,
  rinsed and drained

150 g (5 oz) self-raising flour

75 g (3 oz) vegetable suet

25 g (1 oz) Parmesan cheese, grated

1 tablespoon chopped oregano,
  to garnish

salt and pepper

1 Melt the butter in a large saucepan on the hob and gently fry the onion for about 5 minutes until softened. Stir in the leek, carrots, celery and garlic and cook, stirring frequently, for a further 5 minutes.

2 Add the plain flour and cook for 1 minute. Gradually blend in the stock and cook, stirring, for 5 minutes or until slightly thickened. Stir in the pesto and beans. Turn the mixture into a casserole dish, cover with foil and place on the lower rack of the halogen oven.

3 Set the temperature to 225°C (437°F) and cook for about 30 minutes until the vegetables are almost tender.

4 Meanwhile, in a bowl mix together the self-raising flour, suet, Parmesan and oregano. Season to taste with salt and pepper. Add about 125 ml (4 fl oz) water and mix with a round-bladed knife to form a soft dough, adding a little more water if the dough feels dry.

5 Place dessertspoonfuls of the dumpling mixture over the stew and re-cover with foil. Cook for a further 20 minutes or until the dumplings are light and fluffy. Serve garnished with chopped oregano.

Potato and thyme cakes

Serves 4
Preparation time 20 minutes
Cooking time 30 minutes

1 kg (2 lb) floury potatoes

2 eggs

200 g (7 oz) mature Cheddar
  cheese, grated

1 tablespoon chopped thyme,
  plus extra to garnish

flour, for dusting

6 tablespoons vegetable oil

salt and pepper

rocket salad, to serve

1 Cook the potatoes in a large saucepan of boiling, lightly salted water until tender. Drain thoroughly and return to the saucepan. Mash well until smooth and leave to cool slightly.

2 Beat the eggs, cheese and thyme into the potatoes and season to taste with salt and pepper. Dust your hands with flour and shape large dessertspoonfuls of the mixture into patties.

3 Pour a thin film of oil into a shallow roasting tin and place it on the upper rack of the halogen oven.

4 Set the temperature to 250°C (482°F) and cook for 3 minutes to heat the oil. Add the potato cakes, spacing them slightly apart. (You will need to cook the potato cakes in batches.) Cook for 3 minutes or until lightly browned, then turn the cakes with a fish slice and cook for a further 2–3 minutes. Keep them warm while you cook the remainder. Serve garnished with chopped thyme and accompanied with rocket salad.

Stilton and leek gratin

Serves 3–4
Preparation time 15 minutes
Cooking time 35 minutes

100 g (3½ oz) butter

3 large leeks, trimmed and sliced

100 g (3½ oz) plain flour

25 g (1 oz) Parmesan or pecorino
  cheese, grated

150 g (5 oz) Stilton cheese,
  crumbled

1 tablespoon capers

150 ml (¼ pint) single cream

salt and pepper

spinach and watercress salad,
  to serve

1 Put 25 g (1 oz) of the butter in a shallow ovenproof dish and place it on the lower rack of the halogen oven.

2 Set the temperature to 200°C (392°F) and heat for 3 minutes until the butter has melted. Add the leeks, turning them in the melted butter, and cook for a further 10 minutes, stirring frequently until softened.

3 Meanwhile, put the flour in a food processor or blender with the remaining butter and blend until the mixture resembles breadcrumbs. Add the Parmesan or pecorino, a little salt and plenty of pepper and blend lightly to mix.

4 Scatter the Stilton and capers over the leeks and drizzle with the cream. Sprinkle the crumble mixture over the top. Reduce the temperature to 175°C (347°F) and cook for about 20 minutes until the topping is golden and the leeks are tender. Serve with a spinach and watercress salad.

Pumpkin and green chilli curry

Serves 4
Preparation time 20 minutes
Cooking time 35 minutes

flesh of ½ coconut

2.5 cm (1 inch) piece of fresh root
   ginger, chopped

3 garlic cloves, chopped

½ teaspoon ground turmeric

1 tablespoon caster sugar

1 tablespoon lime juice

750 g (1½ lb) pumpkin, deseeded
   and skin removed

2 green chillies, deseeded and
   thinly sliced

25 g (1 oz) butter

1 large onion, thinly sliced

2 tablespoons toasted pumpkin
   seeds

salt and pepper

To serve

naan bread

mango chutney

1 Chop the coconut into small pieces and put them in a food processor or blender with 275 ml (9 fl oz) very hot water. Blend until the coconut is finely grated. Transfer to a bowl and leave to stand for 10 minutes.

2 Put the ginger, garlic, turmeric, sugar and lime juice in the food processor. Strain the coconut-infused water through a sieve and add the water to the processor, discarding the pulp. Blend until smooth.

3 Cut the pumpkin flesh into small pieces and put them in a casserole dish. Add the chillies and pour in the coconut mixture from the processor. Cover with foil and place on the lower rack of the halogen oven.

4 Set the temperature to 200°C (392°F) and cook for about 30 minutes until the pumpkin is tender.

5 Meanwhile, melt the butter in a frying pan on the hob and gently fry the onion for 8–10 minutes until soft. Stir the onion into the curry and cook for a further 5 minutes.

6 Check the seasoning and scatter with pumpkin seeds. Serve the curry with plain or flavoured warm naan bread and mango chutney.

Spiced veggie burgers

Serves 4

Preparation time 15 minutes, plus chilling

Cooking time 5–10 minutes

100 g (3½ oz) couscous

2 tablespoons olive oil

1 small onion, finely chopped

2 garlic cloves, finely chopped

1 red chilli, deseeded and finely chopped

1 teaspoon cumin seeds

½ teaspoon ground coriander

410 g (13¼ oz) can cannellini beans, rinsed and drained

2 tablespoons roughly chopped coriander leaves

grated rind of 1 lemon

1 egg, beaten

salt and pepper

To serve

crusty buns

green salad

sweet chilli sauce or ketchup

1 Cook the couscous according to the instructions on the packet.

2 Meanwhile, heat the oil in a frying pan on the hob and cook the onion, garlic and chilli over a medium heat for 4–5 minutes. Add the cumin seeds and coriander and cook for a further 1 minute.

3 Tip the beans into a large bowl and mash to form a coarse paste. Stir in the onion mixture, couscous, coriander leaves, lemon rind and beaten egg. Season to taste with salt and pepper.

4 Divide the mixture into 4 equal pieces and form each into a patty. Cover with foil and transfer to the refrigerator for a couple of hours.

5 Put the patties on a baking sheet and place on the upper rack of the halogen oven. Set the temperature to 200°C (392°F) and cook for 5–10 minutes.

6 Serve the patties between split crusty buns with a fresh green salad and sweet chilli sauce or ketchup.

Vegetarian moussaka

Serves 6
Preparation time 15 minutes
Cooking time 40–45 minutes

500 g (1 lb) potatoes, cut into thick
   slices
1 aubergine, sliced
1 onion, chopped
2 garlic cloves, crushed
2 red peppers, cored, deseeded and
   sliced
2 tablespoons thyme or marjoram
   leaves
4 tablespoons olive oil
300 g (10 oz) cherry tomatoes
250 g (8 oz) passata
250 g (8 oz) feta cheese, sliced
300 ml (½ pint) natural yogurt
3 eggs
25 g (1 oz) Parmesan cheese, grated

To serve
garlic bread
green salad

1 Put the potatoes in a large saucepan of boiling, lightly salted water and cook for 5 minutes. Drain and arrange the slices on 2 baking sheets with the aubergine, onion, garlic and red peppers. Sprinkle over the herbs, drizzle with oil and place on the lower rack of the halogen oven.

2 Set the temperature to 200°C (392°F) and cook for 20 minutes, turning halfway through the cooking time. Add the tomatoes after 15 minutes' cooking time.

3 Transfer half the vegetables to a casserole dish and spoon over half the passata and all the feta. Top with the remaining vegetables and passata.

4 Mix together the yogurt, eggs and Parmesan and pour the mixture over the vegetables. Cover the casserole dish with foil, place on the lower rack of the halogen oven and cook, still at 200°C (392°F), for 20–25 minutes, removing the foil for the last 5 minutes to brown the top.

5 Serve the moussaka with warm garlic bread and a crisp green salad.

Chickpea and pepper chilli

Serves 4
Preparation time 20 minutes
Cooking time 1 hour

3 tablespoons olive oil

1 large onion, chopped

2 celery sticks, chopped

2 courgettes, chopped

2 red peppers, cored, deseeded
   and chopped

3 garlic cloves, crushed

2 teaspoons dried oregano

2 teaspoons cumin seeds, lightly
   crushed

400 g (13 oz) can chickpeas, rinsed
   and drained

800 g (1 lb 10 oz) can plum
   tomatoes

2 tablespoons black treacle

1 tablespoon wine vinegar

salt and pepper

To serve
rice
soured cream
chopped coriander

1 Heat the oil in a frying pan on the hob and add the onion and celery. Fry gently for 5 minutes, then add the courgettes, peppers, garlic, oregano and cumin. Fry gently for a further 5 minutes. Turn into a casserole dish and stir in the chickpeas.

2 Tip the tomatoes into the frying pan and add the treacle and vinegar. Bring to the boil and add to the casserole dish, stirring the ingredients to combine. Place the casserole dish on the lower rack of the halogen oven.

3 Set the temperature to 200°C (392°F) and cook for 50 minutes until thick and pulpy. Check the seasoning and serve in bowls over a bed of steamed rice. Top with spoonfuls of soured cream and scatter with chopped coriander leaves.

Cherry tomato and pepper tart

Serves 4
Preparation time 10 minutes
Cooking time 20 minutes

375 g (12 oz) puff pastry (thawed if frozen)

flour, for dusting

oil, for greasing

4 tablespoons red pesto

300 g (10 oz) cherry tomatoes, halved

150 g (5 oz) mixed roasted peppers, roughly chopped

100 g (3½ oz) feta cheese, crumbled

salt and pepper

basil leaves, to garnish

1 Thinly roll out the pastry on a lightly floured surface and cut out a circle 25 cm (10 inch) across. Place on a lightly oiled baking sheet. Use the tip of a sharp knife to make a shallow cut all the way round about 1 cm (½ inch) from the edge.

2 In a bowl mix together the pesto, tomatoes, peppers and feta. Spread the mixture in an even layer over the pastry, making sure the filling is contained within the scored rim. Season to taste with salt and pepper. Place on the upper rack of the halogen oven.

3 Set the temperature to 225°C (437°F) and cook for 20 minutes until the pastry is puffed and golden. Cover the tart with foil if the pastry starts to turn too brown. Serve scattered with basil leaves.

Pasta and pizzas

Tuna rigatoni bake

Serves 4
Preparation time 15 minutes
Cooking time about
  30 minutes

200 g (7 oz) dried rigatoni

2 tablespoons olive oil

2 courgettes, thinly sliced

200 g (7 oz) can tuna, drained

225 g (7½ oz) cottage cheese

400 g (13 oz) can chopped tomatoes

2 tablespoons sun-dried tomato
  paste

1 teaspoon caster sugar

75 g (3 oz) fontina or Cheddar
  cheese, grated

salt and pepper

green salad, to serve

1 Cook the pasta in a large saucepan of boiling, lightly salted water for about 8 minutes or until just tender. Drain.

2 Meanwhile, heat the oil in a frying pan on the hob and gently fry the courgettes, turning frequently, for about 5 minutes until they begin to colour.

3 Break up the tuna into chunky pieces and mix in a bowl with the cottage cheese. In a separate bowl mix together the tomatoes, tomato paste and sugar. Season to taste with salt and pepper.

4 Scatter half the pasta into a shallow ovenproof dish and arrange a layer of the tuna mixture, then the courgettes on top. Spoon over half the tomatoes. Repeat the layering with the remaining ingredients, finishing with tomatoes.

5 Sprinkle over the cheese, cover with foil and place on the lower rack of the halogen oven.

6 Set the temperature to 200°C (392°F) and cook for 15 minutes. Remove the foil and cook for a further 5–10 minutes until lightly browned. Serve with a fresh green salad.

Spinach and ricotta cannelloni

Serves 4
Preparation time 30 minutes
Cooking time 25–30 minutes

12 cannelloni tubes

300 g (10 oz) spinach

75 g (3 oz) Parma ham, chopped

200 g (7 oz) ricotta cheese

plenty of freshly grated nutmeg

350 g (11½ oz) ready-made
   béchamel sauce

50 g (2 oz) Parmesan cheese, grated

15 g (½ oz) breadcrumbs

salt and pepper

1 Cook the cannelloni in a large saucepan of boiling, lightly salted water for 8–10 minutes or until just tender. Drain.

2 Meanwhile, pack the spinach into a large saucepan and drizzle over 1 tablespoon water. Cover and cook for 2–3 minutes until wilted. Drain thoroughly and turn into a bowl. Add the Parma ham, ricotta, nutmeg and seasoning and mix well.

3 Carefully spoon the mixture into the pasta tubes and arrange them in a shallow ovenproof dish. Spoon the sauce over the pasta and sprinkle with the Parmesan and breadcrumbs. Place on the upper rack of the halogen oven.

4 Set the temperature to 200°C (392°F) and cook for 15–20 minutes until the cheese is melting and lightly browned.

Chorizo and olive linguine

Serves 2
Preparation time 10 minutes
Cooking time 15–20 minutes

2 tablespoons olive oil

75 g (3 oz) chorizo sausage, diced

1 garlic clove, crushed

100 g (3½ oz) can butter beans, rinsed and drained

75 g (3 oz) pitted black olives, roughly chopped

1 teaspoon Tabasco sauce

12 cherry tomatoes, halved

125 g (4 oz) dried linguini

50 g (2 oz) Manchego cheese, grated

salt

1 Put the oil and chorizo in a small roasting tin and place on the upper rack of the halogen oven. Set the temperature to 200°C (392°F) and cook for 5 minutes, stirring once.

2 Add the garlic, beans, olives, Tabasco sauce, tomatoes and a little salt and cook for a further 3–4 minutes until hot.

3 Meanwhile, cook the linguini in a large saucepan of boiling, lightly salted water for about 6 minutes until just tender. Drain well and return to the pan. Stir in the chorizo mixture and tip into a shallow ovenproof dish, scattering the Manchego over the surface. Place on the upper rack of the halogen oven.

4 Set the temperature to 150°C (302°F) and cook for 5 minutes until the dish has heated through.

Spaghetti carbonara

Serves 2
Preparation time 5 minutes
Cooking time 8–12 minutes

1 tablespoon olive oil

50 g (2 oz) pancetta or streaky
  bacon, finely chopped

2 egg yolks

25 g (1 oz) Parmesan cheese, grated,
  plus extra to serve

5 tablespoons single cream

200 g (7 oz) fresh spaghetti

salt and pepper

chopped chives, to garnish

1 Put the oil and pancetta or bacon in a small roasting tin and place on the upper rack of the halogen oven. Set the temperature to 200°C (392°F) and cook, stirring once, for 4–5 minutes until browned.

2 In a bowl mix together the egg yolks, Parmesan and cream. Season to taste with salt and pepper.

3 Cook the spaghetti in a large saucepan of boiling, lightly salted water for 2–3 minutes until tender. Drain and turn into a shallow dish. Add the cream mixture and tip in the cooked bacon. Stir lightly, cover with foil and place the dish on the upper rack of the halogen oven.

4 Set the temperature to 175°C (347°F) and cook for 2–3 minutes until hot and the cream and egg mixture is lightly cooked. Serve sprinkled with extra Parmesan and chives.

Goats' cheese pizza

Serves 4
Preparation time 10 minutes
Cooking time 8 minutes

1 thin and crispy pizza base

2 tablespoons ready-made onion
  relish

2 tomatoes, thinly sliced

50 g (2 oz) baby mushrooms, sliced

100 g (3½ oz) goats' cheese, thinly
  sliced

1 tablespoon pesto

15 g (½ oz) wild rocket leaves, to
  garnish

1 Put the pizza base on a baking sheet
and spread the onion relish over
the pizza.

2 Scatter the tomatoes and mushrooms
over the top and add the slices of
cheese. Place on the lower rack of the
halogen oven.

3 Set the temperature to 175°C
(347°F) and cook for 8 minutes or
until golden.

4 Drizzle the pesto over the top of
the pizza and serve garnished with
a handful of rocket leaves.

Ham and tomato wraps

Serves 2
Preparation time 15 minutes
Cooking time 10–12 minutes

2 flour tortilla wraps

2 tablespoons tomato paste

200 g (7 oz) cherry tomatoes,
  halved

6 slices of Parma ham, roughly torn

handful of baby spinach leaves

125 g (4 oz) buffalo mozzarella
  cheese, drained and broken into
  pieces

olive oil, for drizzling

pinch of dried oregano

green salad, to serve (optional)

1 Put a tortilla wrap on a baking sheet and spread over 1 tablespoon tomato paste. Add half the tomatoes, 3 slices of ham, half the spinach leaves and half the mozzarella.

2 Drizzle a little olive oil over the tortilla and sprinkle with dried oregano. Repeat with the remaining ingredients to make a second wrap. Place the baking sheet on the lower rack of the halogen oven.

3 Set the temperature to 175°C (347°F) and cook for 10–12 minutes. Serve the wraps as a quick snack or as a starter with a green side salad.

Easy pepperoni pizza

Serves 2
Preparation time 5 minutes
Cooking time 6–8 minutes

2 plain naan breads

200 g (7 oz) ready-made tomato
  sauce for pasta

100 g (3½ oz) cherry tomatoes,
  halved

150 g (5 oz) mozzarella cheese,
  thinly sliced

50 g (2 oz) pepperoni, thinly sliced

1 tablespoon olive oil

salt and pepper

handful of basil leaves, to garnish

1 Put the naan breads in a shallow roasting tin and spread with the tomato sauce.

2 Scatter over the tomatoes, mozzarella and pepperoni. Drizzle with the oil and season to taste with salt and pepper. Place the tin on the upper rack of the halogen oven.

3 Set the temperature to 200°C (392°F) and cook for 6–8 minutes until the cheese is melting. Serve scattered with basil leaves.

Gorgonzola and rocket pizza

Serves 4

Preparation time 25 minutes, plus proving

Cooking time 35 minutes

250 g (8 oz) strong white flour, plus extra for dusting

2½ teaspoons fast-action dried yeast

1 teaspoon salt

3 tablespoons olive oil

Topping

2 tablespoons olive oil

1 onion, chopped

2 garlic cloves, crushed

400 g (13 oz) can chopped tomatoes

2 tablespoons sun-dried tomato paste

2 tablespoons pesto

1 teaspoon mixed dried herbs

250 g (8 oz) Gorgonzola cheese

salt and pepper

To serve

rocket leaves

balsamic vinegar

1 Make the dough. In a bowl mix together the flour, yeast, salt and oil and add 125 ml (4 fl oz) hand-hot water. Mix with a round-bladed knife to make a dough, adding a dash more water if the mixture feels dry.

2 Turn out the dough on to a lightly floured surface and knead for about 10 minutes until smooth and elastic. Place in a lightly oiled bowl, cover with clingfilm and leave to rise in a warm place for about 1 hour or until doubled in size.

3 Prepare the topping. Heat the oil in a frying pan on the hob and gently fry the onion for 5 minutes. Stir in the garlic, tomatoes, tomato paste, pesto and herbs. Season to taste with salt and pepper and cook for about 15 minutes until thickened.

4 Lightly oil a pizza tray. Tip the dough out on to a lightly floured surface and roll out to a round slightly smaller than the tray. Transfer to the tray and spread the tomato topping over the surface. Crumble the Gorgonzola over the topping. Place on the upper rack of the halogen oven.

5 Set the temperature to 200°C (392°F) and cook for 15 minutes. Serve scattered with rocket leaves and drizzled with balsamic vinegar.

Side dishes and accompaniments

Garlic and pepper roasted potatoes

Serves 4

Preparation time 10 minutes

Cooking time 40 minutes

12 shallots

750 g (1½ lb) small potatoes (such as Charlotte)

2 red peppers, cored, deseeded and cut into wedges

8 garlic cloves, unpeeled

4 tablespoons olive oil

small handful of thyme sprigs

salt and pepper

1 Put the shallots in a heatproof bowl, cover with boiling water and leave to stand for 2 minutes. Drain and rinse under cold running water. Peel away the skins.

2 Halve any large potatoes and cook in a large saucepan of boiling, lightly salted water for 8–10 minutes to soften them slightly. Drain and tip into a roasting tin.

3 Add the shallots, red peppers and garlic cloves and drizzle over the oil. Place the tin on the lower rack of the halogen oven.

4 Set the temperature to 250°C (482°F) and cook for 15 minutes. Turn the vegetables, add the thyme and cook for a further 15 minutes or until the vegetables are golden and cooked through.

Spicy sweet potatoes

Serves 4
Preparation time 10 minutes
Cooking time 17–25 minutes

10 cardamom pods

2 large sweet potatoes

3 tablespoons garlic- and herb-
  infused olive oil

½ teaspoon coriander seeds,
  crushed

½ teaspoon cumin seeds, crushed

salt and pepper

spicy dip, to serve (optional)

1 Use a pestle and mortar to crush the cardamom pods and release the seeds. Remove the shells and crush the seeds a little more.

2 Scrub the sweet potatoes and cut them into thick slices. Cook in a large saucepan of boiling, lightly salted water for 5 minutes until softened but not falling apart. Drain well.

3 Mix together the oil, coriander and cumin seeds and a little salt and pepper. Drizzle the mixture over the potatoes, turning the slices until they are evenly coated. Arrange the potatoes in a single layer on the upper rack of the halogen oven. (You will need to cook the potatoes in batches.)

4 Set the temperature to 250°C (482°F) and cook for 3–5 minutes on each side until golden. Keep the potatoes warm while you cook the remainder. Serve as a snack with a spicy dip or to accompany roast pork or chicken.

Roast potatoes

Serves 4
Preparation time 10 minutes
Cooking time 55 minutes

1 kg (2 lb) potatoes, halved
6 tablespoons olive oil
salt

1 Half-fill a large saucepan with cold water. Put the potatoes in the pan, add a pinch of salt and cover. As soon as the water boils, reduce the heat and cook for 6 minutes.

2 Drain the potatoes and shake them in a colander to roughen the edges.

3 Pour the oil into a roasting tin and place on the upper rack of the halogen oven. Set the temperature to 250°C (482°F) and heat the oil for 5 minutes.

4 Put the potatoes in the hot fat and sprinkle with salt. Place on the lower rack of the halogen oven and cook, still at 250°C (482°F), for 25 minutes. Carefully turn them over and cook for a further 25 minutes. Make sure that the potatoes don't burn, covering them with foil if necessary.

Corn on the cob

Serves 4

Preparation time 10 minutes, plus soaking

Cooking time 20–25 minutes

4 corn cobs

125 g (4 oz) butter, softened

1 red chilli, deseeded and finely chopped

handful of chopped coriander leaves

1 Soak the corn in a bowl of cold water for 30 minutes.

2 In a small bowl beat together the butter, chilli and coriander.

3 Cut 4 squares of foil, each large enough to enclose a cob, and place a cob on each piece. Spoon over the flavoured butter, wrap up the corn in the foil and place on the lower rack of the halogen oven.

4 Set the temperature to 200°C (392°F) and cook for 20–25 minutes. Unwrap the foil carefully, retaining the butter to serve with the corn.

Skewered haloumi
in basil oil

Serves 4
Preparation time 25 minutes
Cooking time 10 minutes

50 g (2 oz) basil leaves, plus extra
   to garnish

8 tablespoons olive oil

250 g (8 oz) haloumi cheese,
   drained and cut into 2 cm
   (¾ inch cubes)

1 large red pepper, cored, deseeded
   and cut into pieces

8 chestnut mushrooms, halved if
   large

1 courgette, cut into thick slices

salt and pepper

To serve
rocket leaves
toasted pine nuts

1 Put the basil leaves in a food processor or blender with the oil and a little seasoning and blend until the basil is finely chopped. Pour 3 tablespoons of the flavoured oil into a bowl and add the haloumi and prepared red pepper, mushrooms and courgette, turning the cheese and vegetables until they are coated in the oil. Meanwhile, soak 4 wooden skewers in water.

2 Thread the cheese and vegetables on to the skewers, alternating the ingredients, and place on the upper rack of the halogen oven.

3 Set the temperature to 200°C (392°F) and cook for 10 minutes, turning once, until the vegetables are tender.

4 Serve the skewers on a bed of rocket leaves and scatter over the pine nuts. Garnish with basil leaves and drizzle with the remaining basil oil.

Caramel roasted vegetables

Serves 4
Preparation time 15 minutes
Cooking time 30 minutes

1 small butternut squash

2 small sweet potatoes

1 aubergine

2 parsnips

2 carrots

2 tablespoons olive oil

4 cm (1¾ inch) piece of fresh root
  ginger, sliced

40 g (1½ oz) dark muscovado sugar

3 tablespoons dark soy sauce

juice of 1 lime

2 small red onions, thinly sliced

2 garlic cloves, thinly sliced

1 Scoop out the seeds and cut away the skin from the squash. Scrub the sweet potatoes. Cut the squash, potatoes and aubergine into 2.5 cm (1 inch) cubes. Cut the parsnips and carrots into wedges.

2 Mix together the oil, ginger, sugar, soy sauce and lime juice. Add the squash, potatoes, aubergine, parsnips, carrots and onions, turning the vegetables in the dressing until they are evenly coated. Scatter into a shallow roasting tin or ovenproof dish and place on the lower rack of the halogen oven.

3 Set the temperature to 250°C (482°F) and cook for 15 minutes. Add the garlic and toss the vegetables together. Cook for a further 15 minutes or until caramelized. Serve with roast or grilled chicken, pork or duck.

Root vegetable gratin

Serves 8
Preparation time 25 minutes
Cooking time 1¼–1½ hours

125 g (4 oz) butter

3 garlic cloves, crushed

2 tablespoons chopped thyme

plenty of freshly grated nutmeg

750 g (1½ lb) potatoes (such as
   Maris Piper)

450 g (14½ oz) carrots

400 g (13 oz) celeriac

300 g (10 oz) swede

100 ml (3½ fl oz) hot vegetable or
   chicken stock

salt and pepper

1 Melt the butter in a small saucepan on the hob and stir in the garlic, thyme and nutmeg. Season to taste with salt and pepper.

2 Slice the potatoes, carrots, celeriac and swede as thinly as possible. (A food processor with a slicer attachment or a mandolin slicer is ideal.) Layer the vegetables in an ovenproof dish, drizzling over a little of the flavoured butter as you assemble the dish.

3 Pour over the hot stock, cover the dish with foil and place on the lower rack of the halogen oven.

4 Set the temperature to 250°C (482°F) and cook for 1–1¼ hours or until the vegetables feel tender when pierced with a knife. Remove the foil and bake for a further 15 minutes or until the surface is golden. Serve with roast meats or poultry.

Chunky chips

Serves 4
Preparation time 5 minutes
Cooking time 20–30 minutes

875 g (1¾ lb) potatoes (such as Maris Piper or King Edward), quartered

2 tablespoons sunflower oil

sea salt

1 Put the potatoes in cold water and leave to soak for 10 minutes. Drain and pat dry with kitchen paper.

2 Place the potatoes in a large bowl. Add the oil, turning the potatoes to coat evenly. Transfer the potatoes to a shallow roasting tin or casserole dish and place on the lower rack of the halogen oven.

3 Set the temperature to 250°C (482°F) and cook for 20–30 minutes until golden brown and cooked through. Sprinkle with sea salt and serve immediately.

Pilau rice

Serves 4
Preparation time 10 minutes
Cooking time 35–45 minutes

50 g (2 oz) butter

1 onion, chopped

225 g (7½ oz) basmati rice

1 bay leaf

3 cloves

5 cm (2 inch) cinnamon stick

50 g (2 oz) flaked almonds

25 g (1 oz) raisins

600 ml (1 pint) water

1 Heat the butter in a frying pan on the hob and cook the onion over a medium heat until soft.

2 Transfer the onion to a casserole dish and add all the remaining ingredients. Mix well to combine and put the casserole on the lower rack of the halogen oven.

3 Set the temperature to 250°C (482°F) and cook until boiling. Reduce the temperature to 200°C (392°F), cover the dish with foil and simmer gently for 20–25 minutes or until all the water has been absorbed.

4 Drain the rice in a colander if necessary, fluff it up with a fork, remove the cloves and cinnamon stick, and serve immediately.

Chilli parsnip chips
with soured cream

Serves 4
Preparation time 10 minutes
Cooking time 25 minutes

500 g (1 lb) small parsnips

3 tablespoons vegetable oil

½ teaspoon celery salt

1 teaspoon ground cumin

1 teaspoon ground coriander

4 tablespoons sweet chilli dipping
  sauce

chopped coriander leaves, to
  garnish (optional)

soured cream, to serve

1 Cut the parsnips lengthways into
quarters and put them in a large
bowl. Mix the oil with the celery salt,
cumin and coriander and add to the
bowl, turning the parsnips until they are
evenly coated. Transfer the parsnips to
a shallow roasting tin and place on the
upper rack of the halogen oven.

2 Set the temperature to 250°C (482°F)
and cook for about 20 minutes,
turning the parsnips frequently until
tender and turning golden. Brush with
the chilli sauce and cook for a further
5 minutes.

3 Transfer to serving plates and scatter
with the coriander, if using. Serve
each portion with a pot of soured cream
for dipping. Serve as a snack or with pork
or lamb chops.

Breads and baking

Cardamom and sultana teacakes

Makes 9 teacakes

Preparation time 20 minutes, plus proving

Cooking time 15 minutes

12 cardamom pods

450 g (14½ oz) strong white bread flour, plus extra for dusting

75 g (3 oz) caster sugar

½ teaspoon salt

2 teaspoons fast-action dried yeast

300 ml (½ pint) warm milk, plus extra to glaze

50 g (2 oz) unsalted butter, melted

1 teaspoon vanilla bean paste or extract

125 g (4 oz) sultanas

1 Use a pestle and mortar to crush the cardamom pods to release the seeds. Remove the shells and crush the seeds a little more.

2 Put the seeds into a bowl and add the flour, sugar, salt and yeast. Mix the milk in jug with the butter and vanilla paste or extract and add to the dry ingredients. Mix with a round-bladed knife to form a soft dough, adding a little more milk if the dough is dry.

3 Turn the dough out on to a lightly floured surface and knead for about 10 minutes until smooth and elastic. Drop the dough into a lightly oiled bowl, cover with clingfilm and leave to rise in a warm place for about 1 hour or until doubled in size.

4 Tip the dough out on to a lightly floured surface and knead in the sultanas. Cover with a cloth and leave to stand for 10 minutes. Divide the dough into 9 equal pieces and roll each into a ball. Set them, spaced slightly apart, on a greased baking sheet and cover loosely with oiled clingfilm. Leave to stand for about 40 minutes or until doubled in size. (The buns will be meeting at the edges but can be separated after cooking.) Brush with a little milk and place on the lower rack of the halogen oven.

5 Set the temperature to 200°C (392°F) and cook for about 15 minutes until risen and golden. The bases of the teacakes should sound hollow when tapped. Transfer to a wire rack to cool. Serve the teacakes split and buttered or toasted, if liked.

Smoked ham and Cheddar muffins

Makes 12 muffins
Preparation time 10 minutes
Cooking time 30 minutes

225 g (7½ oz) self-raising flour

1 teaspoon baking powder

4 slices smoked ham, diced

75 g (3 oz) mature Cheddar cheese, grated

6 sage leaves, finely chopped

1 egg

50 g (2 oz) lightly salted butter, melted

2 tablespoons grainy mustard

150 ml (¼ pint) milk

1 Line a 6-hole cake tray with paper muffin cases.

2 Sift the flour and baking powder into a bowl. Stir in the ham, cheese and sage until evenly mixed.

3 Mix together the egg, butter, mustard and milk and add to the dry ingredients. Use a large metal spoon to stir the ingredients lightly together until only just combined. Reserving half the mixture for a second batch, spoon the dough into the muffin cases and place on the lower rack of the halogen oven.

4 Set the temperature to 200°C (392°F) and cook for about 15 minutes until risen and pale golden. Transfer to a wire rack while you cook the remainder. Serve freshly baked.

Chocolate sables

Makes 12 biscuits

Preparation time 15 minutes, plus chilling

Cooking time 16–20 minutes

100 g (3½ oz) lightly salted butter, plus extra for greasing

150 g (5 oz) plain flour, plus extra for dusting

50 g (2 oz) icing sugar

1 egg yolk

50 g (2 oz) plain, dark or milk chocolate, chopped

1 Cut the butter into small pieces and put them in a food processor or blender with the flour. Blend until the mixture resembles fine breadcrumbs. Add the icing sugar and egg yolk and blend to form a smooth dough. Wrap the dough in clingfilm and chill for 1 hour.

2 Roll out the dough thinly on a lightly floured surface and use a biscuit or cookie cutter to cut out rounds. Transfer the rounds to 2 small, lightly greased baking sheets, spacing them slightly apart. Re-roll the trimmings to make extra biscuits. Place one batch on the lower rack of the halogen oven.

3 Set the temperature to 175°C (347°F) and cook for 8–10 minutes until the biscuits are pale golden around the edges. Transfer to a wire rack to cool while you cook the remainder.

4 Melt the chocolate in a small bowl set over hot water and use a teaspoon to drizzle lines of chocolate back and forth across the biscuits to decorate. Leave to set before serving.

Iced cherry cupcakes

Makes 12 cakes

Preparation time 15 minutes

Cooking time 30 minutes

150 g (5 oz) lightly salted butter,
 softened

150 g (5 oz) caster sugar

3 eggs

175 g (6 oz) self-raising flour

75 g (3 oz) dried cherries

150 g (5 oz) icing sugar

4–5 teaspoons lemon juice

12 fresh cherries, to decorate
 (optional)

1 Line a 6-hole cake tray with paper muffin cases.

2 Put the butter, sugar, eggs and flour in a bowl and beat with a hand-held electric whisk until pale and creamy. Reserving half the mixture for a second batch, spoon the dough into the muffin cases and place on the lower rack of the halogen oven.

3 Set the temperature to 175°C (347°F) and cook for about 15 minutes until risen and just firm to the touch. Leave in the tin for 5 minutes then transfer to a wire rack while you cook the remainder. Leave to cool completely.

4 Mix the icing sugar with enough lemon juice to make a smooth glacé icing that almost holds its shape. Spread over the cakes and decorate each cake with a fresh cherry, if liked.

Raspberry macaroon tart

Makes 10 slices
Preparation time 30 minutes
Cooking time 30 minutes

300 g (10 oz) dessert pastry (thawed
 if frozen)
flour, for dusting
7 tablespoons raspberry jam
3 egg whites
100 g (3½ oz) caster sugar
1 teaspoon almond extract
150 g (5 oz) desiccated coconut
icing sugar, for dusting
fresh raspberries, to serve
 (optional)

1 Thinly roll out the pastry on a lightly floured surface and use it to line a 23 cm (9 inch) loose-based flan tin. Spread the jam over the base.

2 Put the egg whites in a thoroughly clean bowl and whisk with a hand-held electric whisk until softly peaking. Gradually whisk in the caster sugar, a little at a time, until the mixture is thick and glossy, adding the almond extract with the last of the sugar. Stir in the coconut.

3 Spoon the mixture over the raspberry jam and level the surface. Cover with foil and place on the upper rack of the halogen oven.

4 Set the temperature to 175°C (347°F) and cook for 25 minutes. Remove the foil and cook for about 5 minutes more or until the surface is golden. Remove the tart from the tin and dust with icing sugar. Serve warm or cold, scattered with raspberries, if liked.

Blueberry and apple slice

Makes 8 slices
Preparation time 20 minutes
Cooking time 45 minutes

125 g (4 oz) lightly salted firm
  butter, plus extra for greasing
200 g (7 oz) self-raising flour
175 g (6 oz) caster sugar
2 eggs
2 tablespoons milk
2 crisp dessert apples, peeled,
  cored and thinly sliced
125 g (4 oz) blueberries
clotted cream, to serve

1 Lightly grease a loaf tin that will fit on the lower rack of the halogen oven. Line the base and long sides with a strip of greaseproof paper and grease the paper.

2 Cut the butter into small pieces and put in a food processor or blender with the flour. Blend until the mixture resembles fine breadcrumbs. Add the sugar, eggs and milk and blend to form a dough.

3 Spread half the cake mixture into the loaf tin. Scatter over half the apples and blueberries and cover with the remaining cake mixture. Spread the remaining fruits over the top, cover with foil and place on the lower rack of the halogen oven.

4 Set the temperature to 175°C (347°F) and cook for about 45 minutes or until a skewer inserted into the centre comes out clean. Leave in the tin for 10 minutes, then transfer to a plate or board. Serve warm with clotted cream.

Desserts and puddings

Classic rice pudding

Serves 6
Preparation time 5 minutes
Cooking time 1½ hours

50 g (2 oz) unsalted butter, plus
  extra for greasing
150 g (5 oz) pudding rice
150 g (5 oz) caster sugar
1.3 litres (2¼ pints) milk
2 bay leaves
plenty of freshly grated nutmeg

1 Butter the sides of a large ovenproof dish. Put the rice, sugar, milk and bay leaves into the dish. (The mixture should come no higher than 2.5 cm (1 inch) from the top of the dish because the milk will rise a little as it cooks.) Place on the lower rack of the halogen oven.

2 Set the temperature to 175°C (347°F) and cook for 30 minutes, stirring several times. Dot with the butter and sprinkle with plenty of freshly grated nutmeg. Cook for a further 1 hour or until the rice is tender. Leave to stand for 15 minutes before serving.

Cherry clafoutis

Serves 6
Preparation time 15 minutes
Cooking time 40 minutes

50 g (2 oz) unsalted butter

675 g (1 lb 6 oz) pitted black or red cherries

4 tablespoons plain flour

75 g (3 oz) caster sugar

3 eggs, beaten

450 ml (¾ pint) milk

vanilla sugar, for dusting

1 Use half the butter to grease the sides of a shallow ovenproof dish. Tip in the cherries and spread into an even layer across the bottom of the dish.

2 Put the flour in a bowl with the sugar. Gradually beat in the eggs to make a smooth batter.

3 Heat the milk in a saucepan on the hob until hot but not boiling and pour over the egg mixture, whisking well. Pour the batter over the cherries and dot with the remaining butter. Cover the dish with foil and place on the lower rack of the halogen oven.

4 Set the temperature to 150°C (302°F) and cook for about 30 minutes until the batter is only lightly set in the centre. Uncover the dish and cook for a further 5–10 minutes until the surface is lightly coloured. Leave to cool slightly before serving, dusted with vanilla sugar.

Banana pudding
with chocolate sauce

Serves 4

Preparation time 20 minutes

Cooking time about
  30 minutes

125 g (4 oz) lightly salted butter,
  plus extra for greasing

100 g (3½ oz) caster sugar

2 eggs

100 g (3½ oz) self-raising flour

½ teaspoon baking powder

2 tablespoons cocoa powder, plus
  extra for dusting

2 ripe bananas

100 g (3½ oz) plain dark chocolate,
  chopped

2 tablespoons milk

2 tablespoons golden syrup

1 Lightly grease a shallow pie dish. Put 100 g (3½ oz) of the butter, the sugar, eggs, flour, baking powder and cocoa powder in a bowl and beat with a hand-held electric whisk until smooth. Slice the bananas into the bowl and stir in gently. Turn into the prepared dish, cover with foil and place on the lower rack of the halogen oven.

2 Set the temperature to 150°C (302°F) and cook for about 30 minutes or until the pudding is just firm to the touch. Cover the pudding with foil if the top begins to turn brown.

3 Meanwhile, put the chocolate in a small saucepan on the hob with the remaining butter and the milk and golden syrup. Heat gently until the chocolate has melted to form a smooth, glossy sauce.

4 Dust the pudding with cocoa powder and serve with the chocolate sauce.

Rich pear and almond pudding

Serves 8
Preparation time 20 minutes
Cooking time 50 minutes

175 g (6 oz) unsalted butter, plus
  extra for greasing

125 g (4 oz) caster sugar, plus
  1 tablespoon

3 firm, ripe pears, peeled, cored
  and quartered

2 eggs, beaten

75 g (3 oz) wholemeal flour

75 g (3 oz) ground almonds

¼ teaspoon ground cinnamon

whipped cream, to serve

1 Lightly grease a round, 20 cm (8 inch) loose-based cake tin and base-line with greaseproof paper.

2 Melt 25 g (1 oz) of the butter in a frying pan on the hob and stir in the tablespoon of sugar. Heat gently until the sugar has dissolved. Add the pears, turning them in the butter and cook gently for 5–10 minutes, turning several times, until softened.

3 Beat together the remaining butter and sugar until pale and creamy. Gradually beat in the eggs, a little at a time, adding a little of the flour to prevent curdling. Use a metal spoon to stir in the remaining flour, ground almonds and cinnamon until just combined.

4 Turn the mixture into the tin and level the surface. Spoon the pears on top, cover with foil and place on the lower rack of the halogen oven.

5 Set the temperature to 150°C (302°F) and cook for about 40 minutes or until cooked through. (Test by inserting a skewer into the centre; it should come out clean.) Remove from the tin and serve in wedges with lightly whipped cream.

Brownie pudding

Serves 4–6
Preparation time 15 minutes
Cooking time 40 minutes

120 g (3¾ oz) unsalted butter, plus
   extra for greasing

4 large eggs

400 g (13 oz) sugar

120 g (3¾ oz) cocoa powder

65 g (2½ oz) plain flour

1 vanilla pod

whipped double cream, to serve

1 Lightly butter a casserole dish. Melt the remaining butter in a small saucepan on the hob and set aside.

2 Beat together the eggs and sugar until thick and pale yellow. In a separate bowl sift together the cocoa powder and flour.

3 Use a small, sharp knife to slice the vanilla pod in half lengthways. Scoop out the tiny black seeds and add them to the flour and cocoa powder. Stir to combine. Slowly pour in the cooled butter, mix again and combine with the egg and sugar mixture.

4 Pour the mixture into the casserole dish and place it in a larger dish half-filled with hot water. Cover the dish with foil and place it on the lower rack of the halogen oven.

5 Set the temperature to 175°C (347°F) and cook for 40 minutes, removing the foil for the last 10 minutes to brown the top. The centre of cake should look undercooked and sticky. Serve with whipped double cream.

Vanilla melts

Makes 16 biscuits
Preparation time 10 minutes
Cooking time 12–15 minutes

75 g (3 oz) margarine
50 g (2 oz) icing sugar
½ vanilla pod
75 g (3 oz) self-raising flour
75 g (3 oz) cornflour

1 Line 2 baking sheets with nonstick baking parchment.

2 Put the margarine in a warm mixing bowl and sift in the icing sugar. Beat together to make a creamy, fluffy mixture.

3 Use a small, sharp knife to slice the vanilla pod in half lengthways. Scoop out the tiny black seeds and beat them into the creamed mixture. Add the flour and cornflour and mix to form a stiff dough.

4 Shape the dough into 16 small balls and arrange them on the baking sheets, spacing them well apart and pressing them down with a fork. Cover the balls with foil and place on the upper rack of the halogen oven.

5 Set the temperature to 175°C (347°F) and cook for 12–15 minutes until just golden. Remove the foil for the last couple of minutes to brown the tops of the biscuits.

Crunchy apple crumble

Serves 4
Preparation time 20 minutes
Cooking time 20–25 minutes

675 g (1 lb 6 oz) tart dessert apples,
   peeled, cored and sliced

1 tablespoon lemon juice

75 g (3 oz) caster sugar

50 g (2 oz) lightly salted butter

50 g (2 oz) plain flour

175 g (6 oz) granola

pouring cream, to serve

1 Put the apple slices, lemon juice, 25 g (1 oz) of the sugar and a little of the butter in a saucepan with 3 tablespoons water. Heat gently on the hob, stirring for 5 minutes until the apples have softened slightly. Tip into a shallow ovenproof dish.

2 Put the remaining butter in a food processor or blender with the flour and blend lightly until the mixture resembles breadcrumbs. Add the remaining sugar and granola and blend until the granola is broken into small pieces. Spoon the mixture over the apples, spread in an even layer and place on the lower rack of the halogen oven.

3 Set the temperature to 175°C (347°F) and cook for 20–25 minutes until the topping is cooked through, covering the crumble with foil if it starts to over brown. Serve with pouring cream.

Jam roly-poly

Serves 3–4
Preparation time 15 minutes
Cooking time 1 hour

100 g (3½ oz) self-raising flour,
 plus extra for dusting

pinch of salt

50 g (2 oz) shredded vegetable or
 beef suet

1 tablespoon caster sugar, plus
 extra for sprinkling

2–3 tablespoons water

7 tablespoons raspberry or
 strawberry jam

milk, for brushing

vanilla custard, to serve

1 Put the flour, salt, suet and sugar in a bowl and stir in enough water to make a soft but not sticky dough. Turn out the dough on to a lightly floured surface and roll out to a rectangle about 5 mm (¼ inch) thick.

2 Spread 3 tablespoons of the jam over the dough to about 1 cm (½ inch) from the edges. Brush the edges with milk and roll up the dough, starting from a short end. Pinch the ends firmly together to seal. Brush with a little more milk and sprinkle with extra sugar. Wrap loosely in greased foil and place on the upper rack of the halogen oven.

3 Pour boiling water into the base of the oven to a depth of 3 cm (1¼ inches). Set the temperature to 150°C (302°F) and cook the roly-poly for 1 hour until golden. Transfer to a serving plate.

4 Warm the remaining jam in a small saucepan and drizzle over the pudding, if liked. Serve with vanilla custard.

Index

Acknowledgements

Executive Editor Eleanor Maxfield
Consultant Editor Joanna Farrow
Managing Editor Clare Churly
Executive Art Editor Karen Sawyer
Designer Geoff Fennell
Photography William Shaw/© Octopus Publishing Group Ltd
Food Stylists Denise Smart and Sue Henderson
Production Controller Sue Meldrum